To Scott

Christmas.

Love,

Sue and Roy

To Scott

Christmas 2010

Love

Gran and Tony

Classic Greek Cooking
of the Seven Ionian Islands

FEAST FOR
THE GODS

165 RECIPES

BY Theodore Alexander Fouros

Photographs by Lawrence Maultsby

AuthorHouse™
1663 Liberty Drive
Bloomington, IN 47403
www.authorhouse.com
Phone: 1-800-839-8640

First published by AuthorHouse 5/4/2009

Library of Congress Control Number 2009902880
ISBN: 978-1-4389-7213-8

Printed in China

This book is printed on acid-free paper.

authorHOUSE®

CONTENTS

ACKNOWLEDGEMENTS

This book would not have been possible without the considerable help of my beloved wife, Betsy. She wrote down every recipe as I prepared the food, and checked the measurements. She also helped to choose our photographer, Lawrence Maultsby, styled the photographs, and selected our wonderful art directors, Curt Altmann, Paula Rennis and Maria Pereira.

I would also like to thank our local vendors at the Poplar Grove Farmer's Market in Wilmington, North Carolina for helping us find the perfect organic local ingredients.

Susan from Shelton Farms gets special thanks for all the fresh herbs.

Gene, Tom, and Christy, the Motts Channel Seafood Company, Wrightsville Beach, North Carolina deserve special thanks for supplying us with the freshest seafood possible.

INTRODUCTION

To the best of my knowledge, there are no cookbooks that feature the classic Greek cooking of the Seven Islands. Most of Greece was occupied for 400 years by the Ottoman Empire; therefore, both the Middle East and the Orient have influenced more recent Greek cooking. This book represents the recipes passed down by the housewives of the Seven Islands and has preserved the origins of the true culture and cuisine of Ancient Greece. In fact, this book is true to classic Greek cuisine and has no Middle Eastern or Oriental influences. Ancient Greek food is both intricate and interesting, and very little has been written about it.

This book reflects the classical simplicity of Greek cuisine.

There are more than 2,000 Greek islands. Seven of these islands are in the Ionian Sea, which runs between Greece and Italy. However, when Greeks speak of the Seven Islands, they are referring to Corfu, Ithaca, Kefalonia (Cephalonia), Zakinthos, Kythria, Paxos, and Laphkada (Lefkas or Levkas.). Ithaca is the island that is often associated with Odysseus. Kefalonia is the largest of the Ionian Islands. Laphkada (Lefkas) is 60 miles north of Corfu and is separated from the mainland by a narrow channel only 120 feet in width. A broad causeway now crosses this channel. Corfu is thought to be Prospero's magical isle. The Dorians settled Corfu in the eighth century BC. The island succumbed to the Romans in the first century AD. Barbarians, Sicilians, Venetians, and the French have occupied it.

With the exception of Corfu, these islands have never attracted the numerous tourists who visit the Aegean islands. The Ionian Islands are more difficult to reach. Therefore, most of the islands were not taken over by the Ottoman Empire. The most northern of these islands are only a few miles from Italy. Therefore, these islands have a lively mixture of Western European influence, particularly the Italians, Venetians, and French.

These islands provided a refuge for many of the Greek artists, writers, scholars, and intellectuals from the influence of the Ottoman Empire.

The ever-increasing number of people visiting Greece and the Greek Islands will return home with wonderful memories of the foods they experienced. There are more than 11.8 million Greeks living in the U.S.

The streets of Greece are rich with the scent of garlic, cloves, cinnamon, and allspice emanating from homes and restaurants.

Greek food is healthy. Traditional Greek cooking uses copious amounts of olive oil, which helps to prevent heart disease. Horta (the wild greens grown throughout Greece) are high in antioxidants. The housewives of Greece serve lots of vegetables with every meal that are rich in minerals and vitamins. Garlic is a staple in Greek cuisine and has been used in cooking for 6,000 years.

Greek civilization is more than 4,000 years old. A steadfast adherence to seasonal food makes it the oldest, perhaps purest Mediterranean cuisine. Greece is a utopia where musicians and artists can live like gods.

Greece is essentially a maritime nation, and as a result, Greece has had a history of access to all of the aromatics, spices, and herbs from around the world. The Venetians, the Ottomans, and the Germans have occupied Greece. Alexander the Great conquered the then-known world. Yogurt, raisins, and sesame came from the Byzantine Empire, while Italians influenced much of the cooking. The French brought the concept of salads to Greece in the nineteenth century. Exposure to ingredients and ideas from all over the world influenced the fine dining associated with the Greek culture. Greece has spread its culture around the world.

Greeks are responsible for many of the basic principles of cooking. The sage Orion invented the basic white sauce known as béchamel. Lampriades invented brown sauce. Agres of Rhodes was the first to filet fish. Euthymaus is known for his use of vegetables and salads. The first oyster was eaten in Greece. Greece created the first pastry. Artemidorus produced one of the first cookbooks. Many of the recipes written by the philosopher Archestratus, who loved to travel, are still in use in Greece today.

Greek cuisine is home-based country cooking at its best. The classic Greek recipes in this book have been handed down from one generation to the next. Many of the recipes are simple and preserve the taste of fresh ingredients. Many have not been recorded until now.

One never sees a Greek drinking without eating. Thought-filled conversation is part of every Greek meal.

Food shopping in Greece involves many stops. The outdoor markets offer organically grown vegetables, fresh fish, fruits, and herbs. The displays are magnificent. Meats, cheeses, olives, and dry goods are found in small specialty stores. Shopping can take several hours.

Greek food consists of tangy cheeses, fresh seafood, crusty pies, braised meats, root vegetables, grains, pasta, and beans.

The Association of Greek Olive Oil Producers is made up of artisans not large producers, therefore, much of the Greek olive oil is not exported.

The ingredients in the recipes found in this book are generally available in supermarkets, with the exception of a few special Greek seasonings and Greek cheeses. Most of the recipes are for six people.

INTRODUCTION TO GREEK INGREDIENTS

PHYLLO (PRONOUNCED FEELO) Phyllo is pastry in sheets. It is available fresh at Greek bakeries and also frozen in most supermarkets. The fresh ones freeze well and keep for a long time if well wrapped in moisture- and vapor-proof paper, plastic, or aluminum foil.

The pastry sheets are twelve-by-eighteen-inch very thin rectangles. They dry out quickly when opened and therefore must be constantly covered with a slightly dampened cloth when not being used.

Phyllo is used in layers to make a very light and flaky pastry. It can be used for hors d'oeuvres, for the bottom and top layers of pies—both sweet and savory—and for rich, delicate pastries.

To use phyllo dough, one must brush each rectangle with melted butter before adding another layer.

CORE GREEK SAUCES AND STOCKS

There are several core sauces used in Greek cooking:

- Simple tomato sauce, used in many meat and chicken dishes
- Pungent garlic sauce (skordalia) which is thickened with mashed potatoes, walnuts, or bread and served with fish, beets, cucumbers, and eggplant
- A tart, creamy sauce of eggs and lemon juice (Avgolemono) that is used with many traditional Greek dishes from soups and stews to meats and vegetables
- A white sauce (béchamel)

Brown stock, fish stock, and chicken stock are the most frequently used stocks, and they are best when home-made; however, several companies now make a low-sodium, low-fat chicken stock. In this book, you will find that de-fatting sauces and stocks is a big part of many dishes. Many of the same stores that sell kitchen equipment have plastic cups that make de-fatting easy.

GREEK CHEESES

In the old days in Greece, every family raised goats and sheep; however, beef was not always available. Therefore, the best-known Greek cheeses are from either goat's milk or ewe's milk. Most Greek cheeses were made at home, and the best Greek cheeses are still not exported, because they are made in small quantities at home.

ANTHOTYRI: Anthotyri is one of the mildest Greek cheeses. It is similar to a hard cream cheese. This cheese comes from Crete.

FETA/TELEMES: Traditionally feta was made from goat's milk or sheep's milk. It is known in Greece as shepherd's cheese. Feta is a brined cheese and is stored in barrels. Feta needs to be refrigerated. Recently, the Greek government has announced that no other country can produce a cheese and call it feta, much like the French have protected champagne and Roquefort.

GRAVIERA: This cheese is made from cow's milk. It is a semi-hard yellow cheese. Graviera makes a good grating cheese.

HALOUMI: Made from the curd of goat's milk, it is used in saganaki or eaten with the meal. It is crumbly, sharp, and moist like feta.

KASSERI: Made from ewe's milk or cow's milk, it is one of the best cheeses for saganaki.

KEFALOTYRI: Made from goat's milk or sheep's milk, it is an aged, hard cheese. It can be grated and used in many traditional Greek dishes. It is also used for grilling and eaten with the meal.

KOPANISTI: Kopanisti is a blue cheese that is potted while it ripens.

MANOURI: Manouri is made from the whey of sheep or goat's milk. It is a soft, lemony, sharp cheese.

MIZITHRA: There are two types of Mizithra: an unsalted semi-firm cheese or a slightly salty semi-hard cheese. It is made from the whey. It is frequently made by housewives and used as a sharp grated cheese.

HERBS AND SPICES

There are hundreds of herbs and spices used in Greek cooking. Most are native to Greece, however, a few are imported. The herbs and spices that appear most often in Greek cooking are garlic, capers, cinnamon, bay leaf, thyme, oregano, allspice, nutmeg, dill, parsley, and fennel, along with salt and pepper. Others appear infrequently. Lemon, garlic, and olive oil are the trinity of Greek cooking and appear in almost every dish.

Allspice: Allspice is used in béchamel sauce, meat sauces, and stews. It adds a distinctive flavor that is completely different from Italian stews and meat sauces.

Basil: Basil is not frequently used in Greek cooking; however, every housewife grows it either in her garden or in a pot in the house for its fragrance.

Bay leaf: Bay leaf is native to Greece and is used in red sauces, meat stews, and béchamel sauce, and with meat and chicken.

Capers: Capers are used in many sauces and salads.

Cinnamon: Cinnamon is one of the most used spices in Greek cuisine. It is used in most of the Greek sweets. It is often combined with allspice and nutmeg in meat sauces, meat stews, and tomato sauces to provide a distinctive Greek flavor to these dishes.

Cloves: Cloves are used in many Greek dishes, from moussaka and pistitsio to meat sauces and sweets.

Coriander: Coriander is not a frequently used spice in modern Greek cooking.

Cumin: Cumin is used in sausages and in keftedes and in some meat-filled vegetable dishes.

Dill: Dill is one of the most frequently used herbs in Greek cuisine. You find it everywhere. The Greeks prefer to use fresh dill. It can be found in vegetable stews, in sauces such as tzatziki, baked vegetable dishes, spinach pie, field greens (horta) pies, and salads.

Fennel: Fennel fronds, as well as the bulbs, are used in Greek cooking. Fennel is often found in seafood dishes and goes especially well with shrimp. The bulbs are used as a vegetable and braised.

Garlic: Is probably the most used herb. It is everywhere in Greek cooking. When you think olive oil, think garlic.

It is used to season meats, tomato sauces, meat sauces, and vegetables of every type. It may seem strange, but Greek housewives do not use it in salad dressings. In most dishes where garlic is used, you will also find onions and lemon.

Marjoram: Marjoram is used in salads and pies and to flavor meats.

Mint: Mint is used to flavor many Greek dishes. You find it in spinach pies, with meats, in sauces, and in baked vegetable dishes.

Nutmeg: Nutmeg, combined with cinnamon and allspice, is the trio used to give a distinctive Greek flavor many meat sauces and stews. It also appears in most Greek sweets and in béchamel sauce.

Oregano: Greek oregano has a different, stronger flavor than Italian oregano. It is used fresh and dried. It grows wild in the seven islands and the air is scented with it. It smells heavenly when it flowers. This herb is used with meats, in sauces, in meatballs, and in the traditional Greek salad of tomatoes, cucumbers, and feta cheese.

Paprika: Paprika is used to spice the meats used in souvlaki. Chef Alexis also uses it to season broiled and baked fish.

Parsley: Parsley is one of the most used spices in Greek kitchens. Alexis uses only fresh flat-leaf parsley in his cooking.

Pepper: Black pepper should be fresh ground; it is used in most meat dishes and sauces. White pepper is used in béchamel sauce. Greek food is not generally hot. Red pepper is usually found only in sausages.

Rosemary: Fresh rosemary is used in this book more frequently than it is traditionally used in Greek cooking. It is used in chicken and lamb dishes, often instead of or in conjunction with thyme.

Saffron: Saffron has been a staple of Greek cooking for 3,000 years; however, it is not used often in modern Greek cuisine. Fish soups and stews are the most frequent uses of this spice.

Sage: Sage is often used in poultry and pork dishes. It grows wild on the Ionian island of Zakinthos, where the bees use it to make honey.

Salt: Sea salt is considered a staple in all Greek cooking.

Thyme: Thyme grows wild in Greece. It is one of the most used herbs.

OLIVE OIL

It is thought that the first olive tree was cultivated in Crete in 3000 BC. Olive oil is the oil obtained solely from the fruit of the olive tree (Olea europaea L.), to the exclusion of oils obtained using solvents or re-esterification processes and of any mixture with oils of other kinds. It is marketed in accordance with the following designations and definitions:

Virgin olive oils are the oils obtained from the fruit of the olive tree solely by mechanical or other means under conditions—particularly thermal conditions—that do not lead to alterations in the oil, and that have not undergone any treatment other than washing, decantation, centrifugation, and filtration.

Nowadays, the use of olive oil is no longer limited to areas where the olive tree is grown, and it has come to represent quality cooking almost all over the world. The alteration undergone by vegetable oils when heated for frying is quicker and more intense. The higher the content of polyunsaturated fatty acids (seed oils) and the higher the initial acidity of the oil, the more it alters (It is more stable if it has a high content of natural antioxidants—vitamin E.) This alteration also varies according to temperature and length of time heated, number of times used, manner of frying (in continuous frying, it changes less), and the type of food being fried. (Frying fish, especially oily fish, increases the polyunsaturated acid content of the oil, facilitating its decomposition.)

Extra virgin olive oil: This is virgin olive oil that has a free acidity, expressed as oleic acid, of which not more that 0.8 grams per 100 grams, and the other characteristics of which correspond to those fixed for this category in this standard. The term cold pressed means that cold water was not added to the paste when the olives were pressed. Cold-pressed extra virgin olive oil is considered to be the finest olive oil.

Ordinary olive oil: This is virgin olive oil that has a free acidity, expressed as oleic acid, of not more than 3.3 grams per 200 grams and the other characteristics of which correspond to those fixed for this category.

To retain its properties, olive oil must be kept away from excess heat, air, dampness, and especially light.

FRYING WITH OLIVE OIL

Frying is one of the few characteristics common to the entire Mediterranean area, be it European, Asian, or African, and to the three religious groups, Christian, Muslim, and Jewish. It is one of the oldest methods in existence of cooking food.

Recent investigations have shown that frying is beneficial to the organism being cooked, particularly from the physiological point of view. Because of this, it has extended to areas where formerly it was not as popular. Whether the food fried is digested easily or lies heavily on the stomach depends to a great extent on the type of oil used, the temperature of the oil, and the manner in which the food was fried. Studies undertaken on healthy subjects and patients with gastro-duodenal problems (gastritis, ulcer, liver, and biliary complaints) have shown that there is no relationship between food fried in olive oil and these illnesses.

Olive oil is ideal for frying. In proper temperature conditions, without overheating, it undergoes no substantial structural change and keeps its nutritional value better than other oils, not only because of the antioxidants, but also due to its high levels of oleic acid. Its high smoke point (400° F) is substantially higher than the ideal temperature for frying food (350° F). Those fats with lower critical points, such as corn oil and butter, break down at this temperature and form toxic products.

Another advantage of using olive oil for frying is that it forms a crust on the surface of the food that impedes the penetration of oil and improves its flavor. Food fried in olive oil has a lower fat content than food fried in other oils, making olive oil more suitable for weight control. Olive oil, therefore, is the most suitable, the lightest, and the tastiest medium for frying.

It goes further than other oils, and not only can it be reused more often than others, it also increases in volume when reheated, so less is required for cooking and frying.

The digestibility of heated olive oil does not change, even when reused for frying several times.
Olive oil should not be mixed with other fats or vegetable oils and should not generally be used more than four or five times.
The oil used for frying should always be hot; if it is cold, the food will soak up the oil.

There should always be plenty of oil in the pan when deep frying. If only a small amount is used, not only will it burn more easily but also the food being fried will be undercooked on top and over-cooked on the bottom.

FRYING TEMPERATURES

When heated, olive oil is the most stable fat, which means it stands up well to high frying temperatures. Its high smoke point (400° F) is well above the ideal temperature for frying food (300° F). The digestibility of olive oil is not affected when it is heated, even when it is re-used several times for frying.

TEMPERATURE	TYPE OF FOOD
Medium (260–300° F)	**High water content:** vegetables, potatoes, fruit
Hot (300-350° F)	Coated in batter, flour, or bread-crumbs, forming a crust
Very hot (350-375° F)	**Small, quickly fried:** small fish, croquettes

APPETIZERS

MEZEDES

GREEK MEATBALLS
>KEFTEDAKIA ELINIKA

INGREDIENTS

1 Pound Ground Pork
1 Pound Ground Beef, Sirloin
2 Tablespoons fresh Mint, chopped finely
1 Tablespoon fresh chives, chopped finely
¼ Teaspoon fresh thyme, chopped finely
¼ Teaspoon lemon zest
1 Cup onion, grated
3 Slices of white bread without the crust
Salt and pepper to taste
2 Eggs, beaten well
Vegetable oil for frying

Put the bread in a small bowl and moisten with water. Tear into small pieces. Using a large bowl, mix all of the ingredients together with your hands. Roll the meatballs in your hands into balls about the size of a golf ball. Fry in extra virgin olive oil over a medium-high fire. Drain well on paper towels.

Chef's Tricks:
1. The water you use to moisten the bread should be ice cold. This will make the meatballs lighter.
2. Be sure to keep your hands slightly moist when rolling the meatballs.

Alternatives: You can add either ¼ cup of crumbled feta cheese or 2 tablespoons grated Parmesan cheese to the mixture before forming the balls.

Note: These meatballs can be served as hors d'oeuvres or over pasta in a traditional Greek tomato sauce.

EGGPLANT AND GARLIC SALAD
>MELITZANOSALATA

INGREDIENTS

1 Baguette
4 Tablespoons extra virgin olive oil
1½ Cloves garlic,
1 whole clove left unpeeled
1 Small eggplant (½ pound)
½ Teaspoon fresh thyme,
chopped finely
¼ Teaspoon fresh rosemary,
chopped finely
¼ Teaspoon fresh oregano,
chopped finely
1 Teaspoon coarse sea salt
1/8 Teaspoon freshly ground
black pepper
1 Tablespoon chopped
fresh parsley
2 Tablespoons finely grated
Parmesan

Slice the baguette and brush one side with olive oil. Place on a baking sheet in a 375-degree oven and toast until golden. While the toasts are still warm, rub the oiled side with the cut side of garlic clove half. Set aside to cool.

Cut the eggplant in half. Make shallow cuts into the flesh on the cut side with a small knife. Place on a baking sheet. Sprinkle with the thyme, rosemary, oregano, and sea salt and pepper, then drizzle with olive oil. Place in 350-degree oven, with the unpeeled clove of garlic. Bake until the garlic is very soft. Remove the garlic and set aside. Continue baking the eggplant for a total cooking time of 1 hour. Squeeze the roasted garlic onto a plate. Transfer the eggplant to a plate and allow to cool for 15 minutes or until cool enough to handle. Scrape out the flesh with a spoon. Discard the peel. Chop the eggplant and the roasted garlic and transfer to a bowl. Add the parsley and the remaining tablespoon of oil and stir well to combine. Season with salt and pepper to taste. Top the toasts with the mixture and sprinkle with the cheese.

BABY BEETS WITH GOAT CHEESE
>MIKRA PANTZARIA ME TYRIGIDAS

INGREDIENTS

6 Bunches baby fresh spring beets, either red or gold, washed well
(**Note:** the beets should be about the size of a large marble)
½ Pound fresh goat cheese, at room temperature
1 Teaspoon white wine vinegar
4 Tablespoons extra virgin olive oil

Remove the beet greens and reserve for use another day. In a large saucepan, boil the beets until tender. Remove them and set them aside to cool. Peel the beets. Place the beets in a small ceramic bowl and add the oil and vinegar. Toss them well.

Cut the goat cheese into six pieces. Place one piece of cheese in the center of each plate and surround it with the beets. Sprinkle finely chopped fresh parsley over the plate.

Serving suggestions: This dish can be served as a first course, a salad, or as an appetizer or meze.

FOUR-CHEESE TRIANGLES
>TIROPETES

INGREDIENTS

½ **Cup cream cheese**
1 **Cup Feta cheese, crumbled**
1 **Cup Kefalotyri, grated**
1 **Cup Parmesan, grated**
5 **Eggs**
¼ **Teaspoon grated fresh nutmeg**
½ **Cup parsley or dill,
chopped finely**
½ **Pound butter**
1 **Pound phyllo pastry sheets**

Blend the cheeses together with well-beaten eggs. Mix well. Mix in the nutmeg, and parsley or dill.

Melt butter. Carefully cut the phyllo pastry into 3 equal portions. Refrigerate two-thirds until needed and cover the remaining third with a slightly dampened towel. Remove one sheet of phyllo dough, place on a flat surface, and butter well with a pastry brush. Fold in the long sides towards the middle, making a strip about 2 inches wide; butter again. Place one tablespoon of the cheese mixture in the bottom right-hand corner of the strip and fold into a triangle shape. Continue folding, making sure with each fold that the bottom edge is parallel with the alternate side edges. Lightly brush finished triangle with butter.

Bake them in a 425-degree oven for 20 minutes or until they are golden brown. Allow them to cool a few minutes before serving.

EGGPLANT AND TOMATO SPREAD
>MELITZANES YAHNI

INGREDIENTS

**2 Tablespoons fresh parsley,
chopped finely**
2 Tablespoons extra virgin olive oil
**1 Tablespoon fresh oregano,
chopped finely**
1 Medium onion, chopped finely
½ Cup dry white wine
**4 Medium tomatoes, skinned,
seeded, and chopped**
1 Tablespoon tomato paste
**3 Large eggplants,
cut into 1-inch cubes**
Salt and pepper to taste

In a large saucepan, sauté the onion, oregano, and eggplants in olive oil until the onion is translucent. Add the white wine and cook over a high heat until the wine evaporates. Add all of the other ingredients and cook for 1 hour over a medium-low fire.

FRIED EGGPLANT
>TIGANITES MELITZANES

INGREDIENTS

Vegetable oil for frying
**1 Large or 4 small eggplant,
sliced into rounds about
¼ inch thick**
4 Tablespoons all-purpose flour
Water
Salt and pepper to taste

Wash the eggplants well before slicing. Dredge the eggplant slices in a mixture of flour and water. You want the consistency of pancake batter. Heat the oil in a large skillet over a medium-high heat. Fry the eggplant until lightly golden on both sides. Drain on paper towels.

Serving Suggestions: Serve with a small dish of Feta cheese drizzled with a good quality extra virgin olive oil and sprinkled with a dusting of fresh thyme.

FIELD GREENS PIE
>HORTOPITA

INGREDIENTS

1 Package phyllo
dough, defrosted
1 Stick butter, melted,
or a combination of butter
and Fytini (margarine)

Amaranth
Vlyta
Dandelions
Swiss chard
Baby spinach
Arugula
Chicory

FILLING:
3 Pounds of well-washed greens,
Chopped coarsely
3 Large eggs
4 Bunches scallions, chopped
½ Pound of crumbled feta cheese
1 Small bunch dill, chopped finely
3 Tablespoons fresh mint,
chopped finely
½ Cup fresh parsley,
chopped finely
Salt and fresh-ground pepper

This dish is made with a combination of bitter greens. A combination of three of the greens listed below can be used. In Greece, Dandelion greens are always part of the combination.

Remove the thick stems. Place the greens in a large pot of boiling water until well wilted. Drain well and chop again. In a large frying pan, cook the scallions, dill, mint, and parsley in 1 tablespoon extra virgin olive oil until softened. Remove from the heat, and mix together with the eggs and feta cheese. Add the greens and salt and pepper to taste.

Building the pie:
In a large baking dish with straight sides, place 6 sheets of phyllo and brush sheets with melted butter as you add them. Place the filling in the dish and begin layering the phyllo, one sheet at a time, until you have a total of 6 sheets on top.
Score the pie in pieces, any size you prefer. Leave the pie at room temperature, covered for 1 hour. Preheat the oven to 350 degrees. Bake the pie for approximately 40 minutes or until the phyllo dough is crispy and golden brown.

Serving Suggestions: This dish can be served hot or cold. It is used both as appetizer or a main course.
A tomato salad goes well with this dish.

CHICK-PEA DIP
>HUMMUS

INGREDIENTS

**1 15 Ounce can chickpeas,
drained and rinsed well
1/3 Cup Tahini
¼ Cup cold water
2 Cloves garlic, finely chopped
½ Teaspoon ground cumin
¼ Cup Extra Virgin Olive oil
Juice of 1 whole lemon
1Tablespoon fresh flat leaf
parsley, chopped finely
Salt and fresh ground pepper**

In a food processor, grind the chickpeas. Add garlic, cumin and Tahini and pulse for about a minute. Add the olive oil and lemon juice slowly. Pulsing until the mixture is smooth. Season with salt and pepper to taste. Garnish with a handful of whole chickpeas. Drizzle with olive oil. Sprinkle with chopped parsley.

Serving suggestions: Serve with hot grilled Pita bread.

ZUCCHINI FRITTERS
>KOLOKITHO KEFTEDES

INGREDIENTS

3 Large green zucchini
1 Medium onion,
(chopped finely)
2 Eggs
¼ Cup parsley, chopped
1 Teaspoon fresh mint, chopped
½ Cup breadcrumbs
¼ Cup grated Parmesan cheese
¼ Cup crumbled feta cheese
Pepper to taste
Vegetable oil

Boil zucchini (unpeeled) until soft. Remove and chop finely. Press in a colander to eliminate moisture. Smash the zucchini and mix together with the onion, eggs, parsley, mint, breadcrumbs, and cheese. Add pepper to taste. Make small 3-inch patties. Heat vegetable oil about 3 inches deep in large pot. Using a slotted spoon, carefully place the fritters in oil about 3 minutes per side. Remove and drain on a paper towel.

Serving Suggestion: These fritters can be served either hot or cold. They are perfect for a picnic.

SPICY FETA AND PEPPER DIP
>KTIPITI

INGREDIENTS

3 Tablespoons extra virgin olive oil
1 Red bell pepper, seeds and
membrane removed,
cut into strips
2 Red chilies, seeds and
membranes removed and cut into
strips, or hot cherry peppers
1 Pound feta cheese, crumbled
3–4 Tablespoons Greek yogurt

Heat the oil in the skillet over medium heat and sauté the pepper and chilies for 10 to 15 minutes, or until softened. Set aside and allow it to cool slightly.
In a food processor, blend the oil, pepper, and chili mixture with the Feta and yogurt until smooth. Cover and refrigerate until required.

Optional: Add 1 teaspoon of red pepper flakes if you like the dish very hot.

SPINACH PIE
>SPANAKOPITA

INGREDIENTS

4 Boxes frozen leaf spinach
1 Bunch dill
½ Bunch mint
1 Bunch parsley
2 Bunches scallions
2 Large eggs
½ Pound mild feta
**1 Tablespoon ground
black pepper**
2 Tablespoons extra virgin olive oil
1 Box phyllo dough
1 Stick margarine (melted)

Thaw spinach in boiling water. Frozen boxed spinach is already cooked. Drain and chop. In a two-quart sauce-pan, add olive oil and sauté diced scallions until wilted. Add chopped dill, parsley, mint and pepper. Sauté three to five minutes on a medium flame. Mix together in a large mixing bowl Feta and two eggs. Add the chopped spinach and herbs to the cheese and eggs, a little at a time, and stir so the eggs do not curdle.

Brush the pan with melted margarine. Using phyllo (2 sheets at a time), make 3 layers on the bottom of the pan and brush each layer with margarine. Let the sides overlap the edges of the pan. Pour filling into the pan and spread evenly. Place two sheets of phyllo on top and brush with melted margarine. Add two more sheets and brush. Add two more sheets and brush. Fold overlapping edges over the brush with margarine. Using a sharp knife, wet it under hot water and cut into 2-inch squares. Be sure to keep the knife hot or it will tear the phyllo.

Place in a 350-degree oven for 35–40 minutes. Remove and allow to cool for 5 minutes before removing from the pan.

FRIED CHEESE
>SAGANAKI

INGREDIENTS

**12 Ounces Kefalograviera or
sharp provolone cheese cut into
½-Inch slices
All-purpose flour for dredging
2 Tablespoons extra virgin olive oil
1 Lemon, cut into quarters**

Dredge the cheese slices in the flour. Heat the olive oil in a skillet over a medium heat and sauté the cheese slices on both slides until browned.
Squeeze the lemon juice over the cheese in the skillet and serve immediately.
Serves 4–6

Variations:
1. Coat the cheese in a well-beaten egg and proceed as above.
2. Place ¼ inch slices of cheese without flour or egg in a pan sprayed with olive oil, and run the pan under the broiler until the cheese is browned on one side. Flip the cheese and let the other side brown. Note: It will be easier to remove the cheese from the pan if you allow it to cool a bit.
3. Other cheeses can be substituted, such as Kasseri, kefalotyri, or Parmesan.

Note: The Greeks often pour a little Ouzo over the cooked cheese instead of lemon juice.

OLIVE TAPENADE
>HTIPITES ELIES

INGREDIENTS

½ Cup pitted, oil-cured Kalamata olives
4 Tablespoons extra virgin olive oil
2 Tablespoons medium-sized capers
Juice of 1 lemon
1 Large clove garlic
6 Anchovy filets, packed in oil
1 Tablespoon lemon juice
Fresh-ground black pepper

Put the capers under cold running water for 30 seconds to remove some of the salt. Using a sharp knife, chop the olives, garlic, capers, and anchovies by hand until they are almost a puree. Put all of the ingredients in a ceramic bowl and whisk in the lemon juice, olive oil, and pepper.

Note: A food processor with a metal blade can also be used; however, one must be careful that the mixture does not become mushy.

Serving Suggestions: Serve on slices of warm crusty bread.

Chef's Tricks:
1. To clean garlic quickly, place the flat side of a large kitchen knife on top of a clove of garlic and smash down hard on the knife. This will cause the peel to split.
2. To pit olives, use your thumbnail or a small paring knife to split them open. The pits will slip out easily.

CARP CAVIAR
>TARAMOSALATA

INGREDIENTS
1/3 Of an 8-ounce jar of Tarama*
1 Small onion, finely grated
1 Or 2 cups extra virgin olive oil
2 Large Yukon Gold potatoes,
peeled and boiled, or 4–5 slices of
White bread, trimmed of its crust
Juice of 2–3 lemons

* Tarama is caviar from carp.

Mash Tarama and add grated onion. Add a little of the olive oil and beat thoroughly to a smooth paste. Mash the potatoes (or moisten the bread and squeeze out excess water). Continue beating the tarama mixture, adding alternately small bits of mashed potato or moistened bread, olive oil, and lemon juice. Taramosalata should be beaten until cream-colored. Use a food processor with a metal blade.

CUCUMBER, GARLIC AND YOGURT DIP
>TZATZIKI

INGREDIENTS

**2 Cucumbers,
peeled, chopped finely
6 Cloves of garlic
2 Tablespoons fresh dill,
chopped finely
Salt and pepper
2 Cups Greek yogurt
2 Tablespoons
white wine vinegar
2 Tablespoons
extra virgin olive oil
Cheese cloth**

Peel and grate the cucumbers and put in a strainer over a bowl to drain for about 30 minutes. Wrap the cucumber in the cheesecloth and gently squeeze the liquid out. Place the garlic cloves and salt in a food processor with a sharp blade or puree in a blender.

Remove the sharp blade and use the pastry blade. Add garlic, 1 tablespoon of finely chopped dill, yogurt, cucumber, vinegar, and pepper into the food processor. Blend well. Slowly add the olive oil while the machine is still running. Sprinkle the remaining dill on top of the finished dish.

Cover and refrigerate.

Chef's trick: If Greek yogurt is not available, you can use any yogurt; however, you will need 6 cups. Place the yogurt in a strainer lined with cheesecloth and allow the liquid to drain out until the yogurt is thick.

Variations: You can also add dried mint.

WHITE BEAN AND ROASTED GARLIC SPREAD
>POLTOS APO FASOLIA KE PSITO SCORDO

INGREDIENTS

1 Cup dried small white beans
1 Cup low-sodium, low-fat
Chicken broth
1 Bay leaf
4 Sage leaves
2 Stalks celery, cut into
2-inch pieces
3 Large heads garlic
1 Cup extra virgin olive oil
4 Tablespoons white wine vinegar
or lemon juice

Cut the top off of the whole heads of garlic. Wrap the heads of garlic in aluminum foil and roast in a 350-degree oven for about 1 hour.

Place the beans in a large saucepan with the chicken broth, celery, bay leaf, sage leaves, and enough water to cover the beans by 4 inches. Bring the beans to a boil and reduce to a simmer for 1–2 hours or until the beans are very soft. Remove the celery and the bay leaf. Drain the beans. Place the beans in the food processor and mash them. Unwrap the garlic and squeeze the roasted garlic into the beans. Use a wire whisk to emulsify the oil and lemon juice. Pulse the food processor while adding the olive oil and lemon juice to the beans and garlic mixture.

Serving suggestion: Serve with slices of fresh crusty bread and some olives.

GREEK EGGPLANT ROLATINE
WITH FETA AND BASIL
>ROLOS MELITZANAS ME FETA KE VASILIKO

INGREDIENTS

1 Large, firm eggplant
2 Tablespoons extra virgin olive oil
6 Sprigs basil
4 Ounces feta cheese
2 tomatoes, chopped finely

Preheat the barbeque or grill. Cut the large eggplant horizontally and brush with olive oil. Brush the grill with olive oil and put the eggplant on the hot grill. Do not overcook the eggplant. Set aside to cool. Wash and tear the leaves of the basil.

Place thin slices of the Feta cheese on the eggplant and roll it up. Use a toothpick to keep it together. Sprinkle with basil and olive oil.

Serving suggestions: Serve with chopped tomatoes on top.

CHAR-GRILLED OCTOPUS
>HTAPOTHI

INGREDIENTS

**5–6 Pound octopus, preferably
Portuguese, Italian, or Greek
2 Tablespoons red wine vinegar
½ Cup red wine vinegar
1 Bay leaf
Pinch of Greek oregano
1 Teaspoon fresh-ground pepper
½ Fresh lemon
2 Tablespoons extra virgin olive oil
Salt**

Wash the octopus well to remove any sand. Remove the head and the stomach. Place octopus in a pot without water, because octopus naturally maintains a lot of water. Add the bay leaf and the two tablespoons of vinegar, cover it tightly, and cook on a very low fire for 1½ hours. During the cooking, check it once and add water if needed. You can prick one of the tentacles with a fork, and if there is no resistance, it is done. Let it cool. Add a pinch of Greek oregano, pepper, and ½ cup of red wine vinegar. Refrigerate for two hours. Place the octopus on a medium-hot grill and cook for 4 minutes on each side or until it is lightly browned.

Serving suggestions:
1. Remove from the grill, cut into bite-size pieces, and squeeze with half of a fresh lemon and drizzle with 2 tablespoons extra virgin olive oil and salt to taste.
2. Serve the octopus on top of fresh greens such as arugula or a mix of arugula, finely chopped onion, and strips of roasted red peppers.

Note: Greek oregano is usually found dried in Greek markets and is significantly stronger than Italian oregano.

SOUPS

SOUPA

LENTIL SOUP
>SOUPA FAKIS

INGREDIENTS

**1¼ Cups lentils, washed and
picked over for stones
2 Cloves garlic, peeled and
chopped finely
1 Stalk celery, finely diced
1 Carrot, cut into rounds
1 Medium Yukon Gold potato,
peeled and diced
1 Medium sweet onion,
peeled and diced
2 Bay leaves
6 Tablespoons extra virgin olive oil
Salt
Freshly ground pepper
Red wine vinegar**

Soak the lentils overnight in water. In a medium saucepan, add 4 tablespoons of olive oil, onion, celery, carrot, and bay leaves, and cook until the onion is translucent. Add the potato and cook until softened. Add the lentils and cover with water. Bring to a boil, then simmer for 1 hour or until the lentils are cooked. Season with salt and pepper. After placing the soup in bowls, drizzle 1 teaspoon of extra virgin olive oil and a splash or red wine vinegar to each bowl.

BUTTERNUT SQUASH SOUP
>KOLOKITHO SOUPA

INGREDIENTS

**½ Pound butternut or other
yellow squash, peeled, seeded,
and cut into small dice
½ Pound tart apples, peeled,
cored, and cut into small dice
½ Pound yellow onions, peeled
and cut into small dice
2 Tablespoons butter
1 Tablespoon olive oil
1 Large boiled potato,
peeled and diced
½ Teaspoon nutmeg
2–4 Cups chicken broth
2 Sprigs fresh rosemary,
or 2 teaspoons dried
rosemary leaves, crumbled
2 Sprigs fresh marjoram,
or 1 teaspoon dried
marjoram leaves, crumbled
Coarse salt and freshly ground
Pepper to taste
Fresh rosemary sprigs and/or
marjoram sprigs for garnish**

Cook the diced squash, apples, and onions in the butter and oil in a large skillet over low heat until the fruits and vegetables are soft. Add 1 cup of the chicken broth and the herbs and half of the nutmeg; season and continue cooking for 5 minutes. Puree the mixture and the boiled potato in a food processor or blender, adding enough additional chicken broth to give desired consistency. Strain the soup through a sieve to remove the herbs. Garnish with fresh herbs and nutmeg.

CHICK PEA SOUP
>REVITHATHA

INGREDIENTS

1 Pound dried chickpeas
Salt and pepper
1 Cup extra virgin olive oil
1 Medium onion, chopped
1 Medium carrot, chopped
3 Cloves garlic, sliced
2 Stalks celery,
deveined and chopped
1 Large fresh bay leaf
2 Cups chicken broth

Soak the chickpeas overnight in warm water. Boil them in the same water and discard it. Add 2 cups of chicken broth. In a separate saucepan with 1 tablespoon of the olive oil, sauté the garlic, carrots, onion, and celery. Add to the chickpeas. Add the rest of the olive oil and boil for three hours. About 10 minutes before you finish cooking the soup, add salt to taste.

CHICKEN SOUP WITH AVGOLEMONO SAUCE
>KOUTOPOULO SOUPA ME AVGOLEMONO

INGREDIENTS

1 4-to-5-Pound stewing hen
1 Teaspoon black peppercorns
1 Large carrot
cut into 2-inch pieces
1 Large onion
2 Stalks celery,
cut into 2-inch pieces
1 Bay leaf
Salt and white pepper to taste
1 Cup long grain rice or
small-cut pasta
Avgolemono sauce (see sauces)

Remove the giblets from the cavity. Wash the hen, inside and out. In a large stockpot, put 1gallon water. Bring the water to a boil and add the chicken. Hold the chicken by the wings when you put it into the pot, so the cavity will fill with water and keep the chicken on the bottom of the pot. Add the peppercorns, carrots, celery, and bay leaf. Cover and simmer for 2 hours or until the hen is tender. Remove the chicken. Strain and de-fat the broth. Add the rice. Salt to taste. Continue cooking until the rice is soft. Remove from heat. When the boiling has stopped, add the avegolemono sauce. Return the soup to heat. Serve the soup hot.

Chef's trick: Using a hen enhances the taste of the broth; however, the meat of a hen can be tough. If you want to add pieces of chicken to the soup, you will need to cook the chicken in the broth for 4 hours.

MEATBALL SOUP
>GIOUVARLAKA

INGREDIENTS

**1 Pound chopped meat
veal, lamb, or beef
1 Small onion, chopped finely
¼ Cup raw rice
½ Teaspoon Fresh mint,
chopped finely
Salt and pepper to taste
2 Tablespoons fresh flat leaf
parsley, chopped finely
1 Quart veal stock
2 Quarts water
1 Egg**

In a large mixing bowl, with your hands, combine the meat, egg, onion, rice, mint, and salt and pepper. Make small meatballs about the size of a large marble. Roll the meatballs in the parsley. In a large saucepan, heat the veal stock to a simmer. Drop the meatballs into the broth and bring to a simmer for 30 minutes.

Variation: This soup is also delicious when avgolemono sauce is added.

ROASTED RED TOMATO SOUP
>DOMATO SOUPA

INGREDIENTS

12 Roma tomatoes, cut in half
2 Tablespoons extra virgin olive oil
1 Teaspoon sea salt
3 Medium-size white potatoes
1 Clove garlic, cut into slivers
1 10.5 Ounce can low-sodium,
low-fat chicken broth
½ Medium onion,
peeled and chopped coarsely
3 Tablespoons fresh basil,
chopped coarsely
1 Teaspoon red tomato paste
3 Cups water

Cut the tomatoes in half. Lay them flat in a baking pan. Insert garlic and basil in each half. Drizzle 1 tablespoon of olive oil over the tomatoes. Sprinkle lightly with salt. Leave out for 2 hours.

Put the tomatoes into the oven at 250° for about an hour; check to be sure they don't burn. Take them out and allow them to cool. Remove the peels.

Put 1 can of chicken broth, 1 potato, and 1 teaspoon of tomato paste in a medium pot and add the tomatoes, garlic, and basil. Add ¼ cup chopped basil tied in cheesecloth. Cook for 30 minutes on a low heat.

Remove the cheesecloth bag and put the mixture through the food processor. If the mixture is too thin, add a little milk and reheat to thicken.

This soup can be served either hot or cold. If you are serving it cold, top each bowl with a dollop of thick Greek yogurt and a few basil leaves.

Chef's trick: The author uses a potato to thicken soups like this instead of heavy cream.

ROASTED BI-COLOR TOMATO SOUP
>DIO HROMATA DOMATO SOUPA

This soup, created by the author, will wow your guests. It is almost like magic. If you follow the recipe exactly, you will have a soup that is red on one side and yellow on the other.

INGREDIENTS

12 Yellow tomatoes
12 Roma tomatoes
4 Tablespoons extra virgin olive oil
6 Medium-size white potatoes
2 10.5 Ounce cans low-sodium, low-fat chicken broth
2 Cloves garlic, cut into slivers
1 Medium onion, peeled and chopped coarsely
2 Tablespoons fennel fronds, chopped coarsely
6 Tablespoons basil, roughly chopped
1 Teaspoon red tomato paste (Kyknos brand is best)
1 Teaspoon yellow tomato paste
6 Cups water

Cut the ends off of the tomatoes and insert your finger to make a small hole. Do not break the skin. Insert garlic and basil in each of the red tomatoes and insert garlic and fennel in each of the yellow tomatoes. You need two 9-inch baking pans, one for each color. Drizzle 1½ tablespoons olive oil over the tomatoes. Sprinkle lightly with salt. Let them rest for 2 hours. The tomatoes will become much sweeter as a result.

Put into the oven at 250° for about 30 minutes. Check to be sure they don't burn.

Take them out and allow them to cool. Then remove the peels. Get out two medium-size saucepans. Put half of the onions and half of the potatoes in each saucepan, with 1 tablespoon of olive oil, and cook for 5 minutes over a medium heat. Add 1 can of chicken broth and 1 teaspoon of the tomato paste to each saucepan, red to the red tomatoes and yellow to the yellow tomatoes. Add the red tomatoes and add ¼ cup of chopped basil, tied in cheesecloth, to one pan, and add the yellow tomatoes and 1 tablespoon of the fennel fronds tied in cheesecloth to the other pan. Cook each of them for 30 minutes on low heat.

Remove and put the soups through a food processor separately. Be sure to add an extra ½ tablespoon of olive oil to the red mixture before you process the red soup. This will keep the soup from mixing. If the mixture is too thin, add a little milk and reheat to thicken.

Chef's trick: Cut a piece of cardboard into a six-by-six-inch piece. Place the cardboard in the middle of one of the soup bowls. Be sure it reaches the bottom of the bowl. Into each individual soup bowl, using a ladle and holding the cardboard steady with one hand, put the yellow soup on one side and the red soup on the other. Carefully remove the cardboard divider. Using the same cardboard divider, continue filling the rest of the soup bowls. You should now have a bi-colored soup. Be careful taking it to the table, and it will not mix.

Serving suggestion: Garnish each bowl with a few basil leaves on the red side and a few fennel fronds on the yellow side. You can serve it hot or cold.

SALAD

WHITE BEAN AND ARUGULA SALAD
>ASPRA FASOLIA KE ROCA SALADA

INGREDIENTS

1 Bunch arugula,
washed thoroughly
1 Stalk celery, cut into 2-inch pieces
2 Cloves garlic, smashed
1 Can chicken broth
6 Sage leaves
6 Tablespoons extra virgin olive oil
1 Pound dry white beans
1 Pound cherry tomatoes
1 Red onion, sliced thin
Juice of 1 lemon

DRESSING:

6 Tablespoons extra virgin olive oil
Juice of 1 lemon
Salt and fresh ground
pepper to taste
Mix well and pour over the salad
Add salt and pepper to taste

In a large stockpot, add the beans, olive oil, celery, garlic, and sage. Add water and chicken broth to cover the beans plus 3 inches. Bring to a boil and reduce the heat. Simmer the beans (check to be sure you have enough liquid) until they are soft but not mushy. Strain the beans and remove the celery, garlic, and sage leaves. Refrigerate until cold. In a salad bowl, mix the arugula, tomatoes, red onion, and beans and dress the salad.

BREAD SALAD
>SALADA ME PSOMI

INGREDIENTS

½ **Loaf day-old country bread,**
or French or Italian bread
2 Tomatoes, peeled, seeded,
and cut into ½-inch dice
½ **Cup crumbled feta cheese**
1–2 Tablespoons capers
1 Teaspoon fresh thyme,
chopped, or fresh oregano
½ **Cup extra virgin olive oil**
¼ **Cup red wine vinegar**
Coarse salt and freshly ground
pepper to taste
3 Cucumbers, peeled, halved,
seeded, and cut into ½-inch dice
½ **Small red onion,**
peeled and thinly sliced
1 Bell pepper, red, yellow, or
green, cored, seeded, and cut
lengthwise into thin strips

Cut the bread into ½-inch-thick slices and remove the crusts. Set aside. Mix together in a bowl the tomatoes, Feta cheese, capers, oil, vinegar, thyme, salt, and pepper. In a wide, shallow bowl or large platter, make a layer of bread slices. Scatter the cucumbers, onion, and bell pepper strips over the bread. Pour a ladleful of the tomato mixture over the bread and vegetables. Continue layering until all the ingredients are used up, ending with vegetables and tomato mixture. Set the dish aside at room temperature or in the refrigerator for at least 1 hour. It is important for the bread to absorb the liquid from the vegetable-and-tomato mixture. If the dish seems too dry, sprinkle on more oil and vinegar.

TRADITIONAL GREEK SALAD
>HORIATIKI

INGREDIENTS

6 Ripe tomatoes, cut into 6–8 pieces
1 Cucumber, seeded,
peeled, and diced
1 Medium red or sweet onion,
sliced thinly
1 Green, red, orange, or yellow
pepper, seeded and
cut into ¼-Inch rounds
½ Pound feta cheese, crumbled
or in 2-inch cubes
1 Lemon (juice only)
6 Tablespoons extra virgin olive oil

In a salad bowl, mix together the tomatoes, cucumber, onion, lemon juice, and olive oil. Place the pepper rounds on top and sprinkle the Feta cheese over the whole salad.

Options: Add a handful of Kalamata olives to the salad.

Garnish: Top with 2 sprigs of fresh thyme.

BEET SALAD
>PANTZARIA SALADA

INGREDIENTS

2 Pounds beets with the greens on
¼ Cup extra virgin olive oil
3 Tablespoons red wine vinegar

Remove the greens, wash them well, and place them in a pot of water to boil. The greens are done when they are soft and tender. Coarsely chop the greens. Drain the greens and set them aside. Wash the beets and boil them until they are fork tender. Let them cool. Remove the outer skin on the beets and cut them into a 1-inch dice.
Place the greens in a bowl and add 1 tablespoon olive oil and 1 teaspoon vinegar. Place the beets in a separate bowl and add the rest of the oil and vinegar.

Serving suggestions: Place the greens on the bottom of the plate and garnish with the beets.

Variations: This dish is also served with crumbled Feta to top.

BLACK-EYED PEA AND SHRIMP SALAD
>SALADA GARIDES

INGREDIENTS

1½ Cups dried peas
Water
1 Bay leaf
1 Teaspoon savory
2 Carrots, cut into 2-inch pieces
2 Stalks celery,
cut into 2-inch pieces
2 Cloves garlic, peeled
and smashed
24 Medium to large shrimp,
peeled and deveined
2 Tablespoons extra virgin olive oil
1 Head green leaf lettuce

DRESSING:
1 Teaspoon Dijon mustard
¼ Teaspoon salt
2 Tablespoons minced shallots
1 Tablespoon fresh flat-leaf
parsley, chopped finely
4½ Teaspoons white wine or
champagne vinegar
5 Tablespoons extra virgin olive oil

Whisk together mustard, salt, shallots, parsley, and 4½ teaspoons vinegar in a large salad bowl. Add 4 table-spoons olive oil in a slow, steady stream, whisking until emulsified.

In a large saucepan, add the peas and enough water to cover the peas by 4 inches. Add the bay leaf, savory, carrots, celery, and garlic, and bring to a boil. Reduce the heat to medium and partially cover. When the peas are tender but not mushy, drain and set aside. In an iron skillet, heat 2 tablespoons of extra virgin olive oil. When the oil is hot, add the shrimp and cook until the shrimp are pink on both sides. Add the peas to the shrimp. Sauté with the dressing and serve warm over the salad greens.

ORZO SALAD
>KRITHARAKI SALADA

INGREDIENTS

6 Cups low-sodium, low-fat
chicken broth
1 Pound orzo
2 Cups cherry tomatoes,
either red or yellow
8 Ounces feta cheese
2 cups basil, torn into small pieces
½ Cup toasted pine nuts
1 Cup scallions, sliced on the bias,
both the white and green parts
¼ Cup fresh mint, chopped coarsely
½ Cup fresh parsley,
chopped coarsely

DRESSING:
2 Tablespoons lemon juice
½ Cup extra virgin olive oil

Orzo is Greek pasta that resembles rice in appearance. It is made from fine durum wheat semolina and water.

Whisk together the lemon juice and olive oil.
Bring the broth to a boil and add the orzo. Reduce the heat to medium and cover partially until the orzo is tender but still firm. Remove from the heat, drain, and set aside to reach room temperature. Add 2 tablespoons of olive oil and fluff the pasta with a fork to keep it from sticking together. Add all of the ingredients except the parsley and toss with the dressing. Sprinkle the parsley over the top of the salad.

BEET GREEN SALAD
>PANTZARIA SALADA

INGREDIENTS

6 Bunches fresh young beet greens, well washed

1 Tablespoon white wine vinegar
4 Tablespoons extra virgin olive oil

Be sure to wash the greens well, as they often are quite sandy. In a large saucepan, boil the greens for 10 to 15 minutes or until just tender. Remove and drain the greens.

Mix the oil and vinegar with a whisk and pour over the greens. Toss them well.

Variation: In a large skillet, cook 1 clove of garlic (sliced thin) in 1 tablespoon of olive oil. When the garlic is golden brown but not burned, remove the garlic and add the beet greens. Cover tightly and cook about 3–5 minutes or until the greens are wilted. Remove the greens and add 2 teaspoons of white wine vinegar. Toss well.

Note: True garlic lovers top the dish with the golden slices of garlic.

Serving suggestions: The salad often accompanies fried fish or fried calamari.

Chef's Trick: Most people feel the need to buy large beets and greens. The trick here is to buy the small, young ones so the stems of the greens are tender.

CLASSIC MEDITERRANEAN SALAD
>CLASIKI MESOGIAKI SALADA

INGREDIENTS

1 Head green leaf lettuce, well washed and chopped coarsely or 5 ounces mesclun lettuce mix
1 Medium tomato, seeded and coarsely chopped
2 Large radishes, well washed and sliced thin
½ Seedless cucumber
1 Fennel bulb
1 Tablespoon fresh dill, washed and chopped finely

Remove the fronds from the fennel bulb. Remove the outer leaves. Using a vegetable peeler, make slivers of the fennel bulb. Use only half of the fennel bulb.
Peel the cucumber and remove any seeds. Using the vegetable peeler, make thin strips of cucumber.
In a large glass salad bowl, place the lettuce, tomato, radishes, cucumber, fennel, and fresh dill. Add salt and pepper to taste.

DRESSING:
1 Lemon (juice only)
6 Tablespoons extra virgin olive oil

In a small bowl, add the lemon juice and whisk in the olive oil in a thin stream.

SALAD WITH EGGS AND BACON
>SALADA ME AVGA KE BACON

INGREDIENTS

1 Teaspoon Dijon mustard
¼ Teaspoon salt
2 Tablespoons minced shallots
1 Tablespoon fresh flat-leaf parsley, chopped finely
5½ Teaspoons white wine or champagne vinegar
5 Tablespoons extra virgin olive oil
6 Slices of thick-cut bacon, cut into 1¼-inch pieces
½ Fresh ground pepper
6 Large eggs
6 Cups well-washed and torn frisee
Fresh ground black pepper to taste

Whisk together mustard, salt, shallots, parsley, and 4½ teaspoons vinegar in a large salad bowl. Add 4 tablespoons olive oil in a slow, steady stream, whisking until emulsified. Heat the remaining olive oil in a small frying pan over high heat and brown the bacon with pepper, stirring for 1–2 minutes. In a small skillet, add 2 inches of water and 1 teaspoon of vinegar and bring to a simmer. Break one egg into a cup and slowly slide it into the simmering water. Repeat with the remaining eggs. Poach at a bare simmer until the whites are firm and the yolks are still runny, 2–3 minutes. Remove the eggs and set aside on paper towels. Season with salt and pepper. Toss the frisee with the dressing. Serve on individual plates and top with bacon and eggs.

COLD LOBSTER SALAD
>SALADA ASTAKOU KRYA

INGREDIENTS

6 1½- to 2-Pound lobsters

DRESSING:
6 Tablespoons extra virgin olive oil
Salt and pepper to taste
Juice of 1 lemon
1 Teaspoon fresh tarragon, chopped finely
2 Tablespoons fennel fronds, chopped finely
2 Tablespoons fresh parsley, chopped finely

Using a lobster pot or a very large stockpot, bring 6 quarts of water to a boil. Drop the lobsters into the boiling water, head first. Bring the water back to a boil and cook the lobsters uncovered for 20 minutes. Remove the lobsters from the pot and set them aside to cool for 10 minutes. Roll each lobster on its back. Using a very sharp, strong, chef's knife, split the belly from the head to the tip of the tail. Do not cut all the way through to the meat in the tail. Remove the green mass from the head.

Take the claws off and use a nutcracker to crack the shells. Be careful not to destroy the meat. It should come out in one piece. Twist off the tail and carefully remove the meat so that it comes out in one piece.

Slice the tail meat into ½ inch pieces. Place all of the lobster meat in a large bowl. In a separate bowl, whisk together the dressing. Pour the dressing over the lobster meat and mix carefully, so as not to destroy the meat.

Serving suggestions: Serve the lobster on a long serving dish. Starting with the claws, recreate the look of a lobster with the meat. Drizzle the lobster with extra virgin olive oil and garnish with lemon wedges and fennel fronds.

ARUGULA SALAD
>ROCA SALADA

INGREDIENTS

**2 Bunches arugula leaves,
washed thoroughly
Juice of 1 lemon
4 Tablespoons extra virgin olive oil
Kefalotyri or Parmesan cheese
Salt and pepper**

Trim the stems from the arugula, and wash each bunch three times to remove any sand or dirt. Dry well in a salad spinner or roll in paper towels and pat dry. Place in a salad bowl. Using a vegetable peeler, make thin slices of cheese and place on top of the salad. Pour the olive oil over the salad. Add the lemon juice, salt, and pepper, and toss.

VEGETABLES

LITTLE SHOES
>PAPOUTSAKIA

INGREDIENTS

6 Medium eggplants
½ Cup butter (two sticks)
1 Tablespoon fresh parsley,
chopped finely
1 Cup boiling water
2 Medium sweet onions,
chopped finely
½ Pound of ground beef or lamb
Salt and pepper
1 Cup tomato sauce
(see sauces page 220)
½ Cup grated Kefalotyri cheese
1 Cup Béchamel sauce
(see sauces page 223)

Preheat the oven to 350 degrees. Wash the eggplants in cold water and pat dry. Cut the eggplants in half lengthwise. With a spoon, scoop out the pulp and chop coarsely. Place the shells in a greased baking dish and cook until they begin to soften. In a skillet, sauté the onions, parsley, and eggplant pulp until the onions are translucent. Add the ground meat and cook until the meat is brown. Add the tomato sauce. Simmer until most of the liquid is absorbed. Fill the eggplant shells with the mixture and top each with béchamel sauce. Add ½ cup of water to the baking pan. Sprinkle with grated cheese and put back in the oven until the tops are golden brown.

Variation: Many Greek housewives use mashed potatoes as the topping for these little shoes instead of béchamel sauce.

Note: For this recipe, you will need to refer to the Sauces section for the recipes for tomato sauce and béchamel sauce.

ARTICHOKES, FAVA BEANS, AND POTATOES
>KOUKIA ME AGINARES ME PATATES A LA POLITA

INGREDIENTS

8 Medium size fresh artichokes or
3 15 Ounce cans artichoke hearts
1½ Pounds shelled fava beans
2 Pounds Yukon Gold potatoes,
quartered
2 Tablespoons extra virgin olive oil
2 Bunches scallions
1 Cup fresh fennel, chopped
finely, including the fronds
½ Cup white wine
Juice of 1 lemon
1 10.5 Ounce can low-sodium
chicken broth

If using fresh artichokes, cut the outer leaves off, scoop the fuzz on the heart out, quarter the hearts, and put them into a pot of cold, salted water for 10 minutes. Rinse.

Sauté the scallions with the chopped fennel until the scallions are softened. Add potatoes, artichokes, chicken broth, and a cup of water. Cook over medium heat for 20 minutes, uncovered. After 20 minutes, add the fava beans. Cook until almost all of the liquid evaporates, then add lemon juice.

Serving suggestion: Serve with good quality crusty bread and Feta cheese.

BAKED COLD STUFFED
SUMMER VEGETABLES
>YEMISTA

INGREDIENTS

3 Peppers, green, red, and yellow
3 Large tomatoes
6 Zucchini, 3 green, 3 yellow
3 Small eggplants
3 Cups raw rice
5 Tablespoons olive oil
**¾ Medium bunch mint,
minced finely**
1 Medium bunch dill, minced finely
**1 Medium bunch parsley,
minced finely**
1 Bunch green onions, minced
¼ Cup minced basil
1 Large Spanish onion, minced finely
1 Clove garlic, minced finely
1 8-oz Can tomato juice
3 Cups water
Salt and pepper to taste

Use a large, deep, ovenproof baking dish.

Cut tops off the vegetables and reserve. Scoop out the center of each vegetable and chop finely. Mix together in a large bowl 3 tablespoons olive oil, rice, chopped vegetables and spices. Add ¾ of the herbs. Stuff the hollow vegetables with the mixture and replace the lids. Place in the baking dish. Pour tomato juice, water, and olive oil in the pan, surrounding the vegetables. Place left over herbs in the juice.

Bake in a 400-degree oven for 1 hour.

Remove and refrigerate. This dish may be made 1 to 2 days ahead of serving.

Variations:
1. This dish may also be served hot.
2. Add chopped beef or lamb to the rice stuffing and top the vegetables with grated Parmesan cheese. Brown tops in oven.

BAKED MIXED VEGETABLES
>BRIAM

INGREDIENTS

2 Teaspoons plus ¼ cup extra virgin olive oil
3 Medium onions, sliced
1½ Pounds small white potatoes, peeled and halved or sliced into thick rounds
1½ Pounds zucchini, cut into 1/3-inch rounds
6-8 Roma tomatoes, peeled and coarsely chopped
2 Large green peppers, seeded and sliced into thin rounds
2–3 Cloves garlic chopped finely
1 Teaspoon thyme, chopped finely
¼ Cup fresh flat leaf parsley, chopped finely
2 Tablespoons fresh dill, chopped finely
Salt and freshly ground pepper to taste
¼ to ½ Cup water

Preheat the oven to 350° F. In a large, heavy skillet, heat the 2 tablespoons of olive oil and sauté the onion until translucent. In a medium baking dish, combine the onions, vegetables, herbs, salt, and pepper, ¼ cup of olive oil, and some of the water. Bake for 1½ to 2 hours or until the potatoes are soft and the vegetables completely cooked. Note: You may need to add water along the way to prevent burning. Remove the pan from the oven and allow to cool.

Serving suggestion: This dish is best served with Feta cheese on the side.

Chef's trick: Use a vegetable peeler to remove the harsh outer skin of the peppers.

BAKED EGGPLANT, ZUCCHINI, AND POTATOES
>LADERA LAHANIKA

INGREDIENTS

3 Tablespoon extra virgin olive oil
1 Large eggplant, thinly sliced
1 Large onion,
peeled and thinly sliced
2 Garlic cloves, peeled and diced
1 Tablespoon fresh dill, chopped fine
2 Large potatoes,
peeled and thinly sliced
5 Ripe tomatoes, thinly sliced
6 Zucchini, trimmed and thinly sliced
Salt
Pepper
1 Teaspoon dried oregano
½ Cup water
3 Tablespoons breadcrumbs

Preheat the oven to 400° F. Heat one tablespoon of the oil in a skillet over medium heat. Add the eggplant, onion, dill, and garlic, and sauté for 5–7 minutes or until softened. Place in a twelve-by-twelve-inch baking dish. Place the potatoes, tomatoes, and zucchini in alternate layers on top of the eggplant and onion mixture, seasoning each layer with salt, pepper, and oregano. Pour off the water and drizzle 1 tablespoon of olive oil over the top layer of zucchini. Sprinkle with the breadcrumbs and drizzle the remaining tablespoon of olive oil. Bake the dish in the oven for 45 minutes or until the top has browned and the vegetables are tender.

CAULIFLOWER
>KOUNOUPIDI

INGREDIENTS

1 Medium cauliflower, with the
hard stem and outer leaves removed

DRESSING:
6 Tablespoons extra virgin
olive oil, cold pressed
1 Tablespoon red wine vinegar
or sherry vinegar

Wash the cauliflower well and cut into bite-size pieces. Drop the cauliflower into a pot of boiling water. Cook until it is tender. Set aside to cool. Pour the dressing over the cauliflower and toss.

Place the ingredients in a bowl and whisk together until the ingredients are emulsified.

Serving suggestion: Traditionally, this dish is served at room temperature with fried fish.

LETTUCE DOLMATHES
>MAROULIA DOLMATHES

INGREDIENTS

Select lettuce with leaves suitable for stuffing. Clean carefully and separate leaves.
2 Pounds chopped lamb
4 to 6 Bunches scallions, chopped or 1½ Pounds onions, chopped
2 Tablespoons extra virgin olive oil
1 Cup raw rice (preferably Uncle Ben's long-grain rice)
½ Cup chopped fresh parsley
½ Teaspoon chopped fresh mint
2 Eggs, well beaten
2 Tablespoons butter
Salt and pepper
2 Cups chicken broth
Water as needed

Bring a pot of water to a boil and add the leaves a few at a time. Boil for 5 minutes until they are just soft. Remove from the water and set the leaves aside.

Mix together the meat, rice, mint, parsley, onions, and salt and pepper. Sauté in olive oil until the meat is brown. Allow to cool. Add the eggs and mix with your hands.

Put one to two tablespoons of filling in the center of the leaf and fold the sides up over it, covering it. Roll it like a cigar. Fold over the ends. Lay the stuffed leaves in a pot (open side down so they do not swell open) in even, tight rows. When one layer is completed, make a second and third layer. Lay a plate directly on top layer of the dolmathes. Add enough chicken broth and water to the pot to half cover the leaves, and add butter. Cover the pot. Simmer for about 1 hour until 1½ cups of liquid remain.

Recipe options: Pine nuts or raisins can be added to the stuffing.

Serving options: Usually served cold with lemon wedges. Can also be served hot with avgolemono sauce. (See sauces.)

STUFFED GRAPE LEAVES
>DOLMATHES

INGREDIENTS

1½ Pounds tender grape leaves
1½ Pounds onions, chopped
2 Tablespoons extra virgin olive oil
1¼ Cups raw rice (preferably
Uncle Ben's long-grain rice)
½ Cup chopped fresh parsley
2 Tablespoons chopped fresh dill
½ Teaspoon chopped
fresh mint leaves
Salt and pepper
1 Lemon, juice only
2 Tablespoons butter
2 Cups chicken broth
Water as needed

Buy the prepared grapevine leaves, and wash them in cold water before using.

Sauté the onions in oil to a very light golden color. Add the rice and brown lightly. Add 1½ cups of water and the parsley, dill, mint, and salt and pepper to taste. Cook 5 to 7 minutes or until the rice absorbs the liquid but is only half-cooked. (Watch it carefully so it does not stick to the pot.)

When filling the leaves, keep the shiny side of the leaf on the outside. Put one tablespoon of filling in the center of the leaf and fold the sides up over it, covering it. Roll it like a cigar. Lay the stuffed leaves in a pot (open side down so they do not swell open.) in even, tight rows. When one layer is completed, make a second and third layer. Lay a plate directly on top layer of the dolmathes. Add enough chicken broth to the pot to half cover the leaves, and add the butter. Cover the pot. Cook for 1½ hours on a medium to low fire.

There should be about 1½ cups of liquid remaining.

Recipe options: Pine nuts or raisins can be added to the stuffing.

Serving options: Usually served cold with lemon wedges. Can also be served hot with avgolemono sauce. (See sauces page 228).

LARGE BROAD BEANS
>GIGANTES

INGREDIENTS

1 Pound dried broad beans
1 Medium onion, chopped coarsely
2 Tablespoons fresh Italian
parsley, chopped finely
1 Tablespoon tomato paste
4 Roma tomatoes, peeled,
seeded, and chopped
1 Clove garlic, crushed and chopped
1 Teaspoon dried oregano
3 Tablespoons extra virgin olive oil
Water to cover
Salt and pepper to taste

Soak the beans in water overnight. Put olive oil and onion in a saucepan and cook over medium heat until translucent. Add the tomato paste, tomatoes, oregano, beans, and garlic. Cover with water. Add salt and pepper and bring to a boil for 15 minutes and empty them into a baking dish. Sprinkle with parsley and bake at 350° for 45 minutes. Check to see if you need additional liquid.

FETA STUFFED TOMATOES
>TOMATES GEMISTES ME FETA

INGREDIENTS

6 Ripe, medium-sized tomatoes
¼ Cup crumbled feta cheese
1 Tablespoon fresh thyme,
chopped finely

Bring the cheese to room temperature. Wash the tomatoes under cold water. Remove the area where the stem was. Turn the tomatoes upside down and squeeze out the seeds. Be careful not to break the skin. Remove some of the interior. Mix together the cheese and the thyme. Put a dollop of the cheese mixture in each tomato.

Place the tomatoes on a baking dish and put them under the broiler for 5 minutes or until the cheese is browned on top.

Serving suggestions: This dish goes well with any grilled meat or fish. It is often served with French fries.

GARLIC MASHED POTATOES
>POURE APO PATATES, KE SKORDO

INGREDIENTS

**1 Whole head garlic
6 Large Yukon Gold potatoes
1 Teaspoon salt
Fresh-ground white pepper
1 Stick butter**

Wrap a whole head of garlic in foil and put it in a skillet in a preheated oven at 400 degrees for 30 minutes. Remove the foil and cut the top off. Allow it to cool.
Peel the potatoes. Bring them to a boil in a large pot. Cook the potatoes for 20 minutes or until they are soft in the middle. Drain them.
Place each potato in a ricer and squeeze into a large bowl. Add the butter, salt, and pepper, and mix well. If the potatoes are a bit thick, add extra virgin olive oil until you have the desired consistency. When the garlic is easy to handle, squeeze the roasted garlic into the potato mixture. Mix well.

FRESH ENGLISH PEAS WITH DILL
>BIZELIA ME MARATHO

INGREDIENTS

**3 Pounds fresh English
peas, shelled
½ Bunch fresh dill, washed well
1 Large leek, outer leaves and the
green top removed
1 Cup low-sodium, low-fat
chicken broth
1¼ Sticks butter**

In a large saucepan, cook the dill, leek, and peas in a cup of chicken broth until the peas are soft but still bright green. Remove the dill and the leek and drain the peas. Put the peas in a bowl and immerse them in an ice water bath to stop the cooking. In a small frying pan, brown the butter. Drain the peas and pour the brown butter over them.

Serving suggestions: This dish is served with fish or meats.

FRIED POTATOES
>TIGANITES PATATES

INGREDIENTS

6 Large russet potatoes
2 Quarts vegetable oil or a mix of olive oil and vegetable oil
Sea salt

While many people consider French fries a French dish, they are a staple at any Greek table. They are served as meze or as a side dish.

Peel the potatoes and cut each one lengthwise into ¼-inch-thick slices.

Chef's trick: Place the potatoes in a large bowl of water and refrigerate for at least 1 hour. This process removes the excess starch and makes for very crispy fries. Drain the potatoes and pat dry on paper towels.
In a large skillet, heat the oil to 370 degrees. Try to keep the temperature medium hot. Begin the process of frying. Remove the potatoes when they become a golden brown, and drain them on paper towels. Sprinkle with sea salt.

Variations: Cut the potatoes into 1-inch cubes and prepare as above.

OLIVE OIL ROASTED SMASHED POTATOES
>POURE PATATAS ME LADI

INGREDIENTS

6 Large Yukon Gold potatoes
1 Teaspoon salt
Fresh-ground white pepper
¼ Cup extra virgin olive oil

Wash and wrap each potato in foil. Place them in a 400-degree oven for 1 hour. Remove and let them cool. Peel the potatoes. Place each potato in a ricer and squeeze into a large bowl. Add the olive oil, salt and pepper and mix well. If the potatoes are a bit thick, add a little milk until you have the desired consistency.

GREEN BEANS WITH
RED PEPPERS AND MUSHROOMS
>FRESCA FASOULIA ME PIPERIES KE MANITARIA

INGREDIENTS

1 Pound green beans
4 Large mushrooms
½ Large red pepper
2 Tablespoons vegetable oil
1 Tablespoon balsamic vinegar

Cut the ends from the green beans. Slice the mushrooms thin. Remove the stem and seeds from the red pepper and cut into thin strips.

In a wok, pour the vegetable oil and add 1 clove of garlic. On a high heat, brown the garlic. Do not allow it to burn. Remove garlic. Add red pepper, green beans, and mushrooms. Cook until slightly tender. Do not overcook. Add balsamic vinegar. Toss together for 1 minute.

EGGPLANT CASSEROLE
>MOUSSAKA

This is a four-step recipe calling for making a meat sauce, preparing the eggplants, and making a béchamel sauce. Start by making the meat sauce, then prepare the eggplants and lastly, make the béchamel sauce.

MEAT SAUCE/KYMAS
(see sauces page 219)

Step 1: Make one recipe of meat sauce.

GRILLED EGGPLANTS AND POTATOES INGREDIENTS

3 Large eggplants, sliced round and about 1/3 inch thick
3 Large oval Idaho potatoes, peeled and cut lengthwise into 1/3-inch slices
Salt
½ Cup extra virgin olive oil

Step 2: Grill eggplants and potatoes. Wash the eggplants and cut off the stems and tips. Cut into large oval slices, about 1/3 inch thick. Place in a bowl and sprinkle liberally with salt. Allow to rest for 45 minutes to 1 hour. Rinse the slices well and drain. Peel and slice the potatoes. Let soak in cold water for 15 minutes. Pat vegetables dry with paper towels. In the old days, the eggplant and the potatoes were fried; however, we prefer to grill them. In a small bowl, put ½ cup olive oil. Using a pastry brush, coat both sides of the eggplant and potato slices and place on a medium grill. When they are lightly browned on both sides, remove from the grill and set aside.
If grilling is not an option, you can place the vegetables on an un-greased baking pan and broil until golden brown. Set aside to cool.

Variation: Zucchini can be used instead of the eggplants.

BÉCHAMEL SAUCE
4-6 Cups Béchamel sauce
(see sauces pag 223)
1 cup grated Kefalotyri or Parmesan cheese
½ cup plain breadcrumbs (not seasoned)

Serves: 8-10 people

STEP 3: Make two recipes of Bechamel sauce

STEP 4: PUT THE DISH TOGETHER: Preheat the oven to 350° F. Lightly oil an eleven-by-fifteen-by-three-inch baking pan, Pyrex, or ceramic dish. Sprinkle breadcrumbs lightly on the bottom of the baking dish. Begin to make layers, first the eggplant and potatoes—which should be overlapped—then the meat sauce. Sprinkle with cheese. Keep making layers until you have used up the vegetables. Set aside to cool. Gently pour the béchamel over the top layer. Bake in the oven for 45 minutes until the béchamel is thick and golden brown. Set the dish aside for at least 20 minutes before cutting into individual servings.

LEMON POTATOES
>PATATES LEMONATES

INGREDIENTS

**6 Large russet potatoes, peeled and
cut lengthwise into 6 pieces each
3 Stalks fresh celery,
cut into 4-Inch pieces
1 10.5 Ounce can low-sodium,
low-fat chicken broth
1 Cup water
Juice of 1 lemon
2 Tablespoons fresh oregano, or
1 Teaspoon dry oregano
2 Tablespoons extra virgin olive oil
3 Tablespoons Fytini or margarine
Salt and pepper to taste**

Preheat the oven to 400° degrees. Place the potatoes in a large baking dish with the celery, chicken broth, and water. Top the potatoes with salt and pepper, lemon juice, and Fytini (margarine) and 2 tablespoons of extra virgin olive oil. Bake in the oven until the tops are nicely browned. Turn them once and brown the other side. Remove the celery and serve.

Option: Some housewives also add several cloves of garlic.

Chef's trick: Soak the potatoes in cold water for five minutes. Pour off the water and repeat. This removes most of the starch and makes the outside of the potatoes crispy.

Serving suggestions: Greeks eat more potatoes than the Irish. It is a staple in their diet. This dish is served with leg of lamb or the whole lamb cooked on the spit, on Greek Easter. It is also served with grilled or roasted chicken.

RICE PILAF WITH SPINACH
>SPANAKORIZO OR RYZI ME SPANAKI

INGREDIENTS

2 Small shallots, peeled and chopped finely
1 Tablespoon butter
1 Tablespoon extra virgin olive oil
2 Tablespoon chopped fresh dill
2 Tablespoon chopped fresh mint
2 Tablespoons chopped fresh flat-leaf parsley
Pinch nutmeg
1 Cup chopped tomatoes
3 Pounds fresh spinach, washed well, trimmed, and chopped
1 Bay leaf
1 Can low-fat, low-sodium chicken broth
1 Cup long-grain rice (Uncle Ben's)
Water

In a medium saucepan, sauté the shallots and bay leaf in butter and olive oil for 1 minute. Add the rice; toast the rice, stirring constantly, for two minutes. Add the chicken broth and water as needed. Add the tomatoes and spinach. Bring to a rolling boil and cook uncovered until most of the liquid is reduced to the same height in the pot as the rice. Add in the other ingredients. Cover tightly and remove from the stove. In a preheated oven, cook the mixture, covered, for 20 minutes at 400 degrees.

Chef's trick: In order to determine the amount of liquid required to cook the rice, add the chicken broth, then a can of water. You may need to add more water. The liquid needs to be two fingers above the rice when you start it boiling.

Variations: Add ¼ cup of toasted pine nuts to the rice when it has finished cooking.

OKRA WITH FRESH TOMATOES
>BAMYIES YIAHNI

INGREDIENTS

**2 Pounds okra, not larger than
3 inches each
2 Pounds fresh ripe tomatoes
2 Tablespoons fresh parsley,
chopped
Freshly ground black pepper
½ Large onion, chopped finely
2 Tablespoons olive oil
½ Cup white wine vinegar**

Cut off the end of the okra where it is attached to the vine. In order for the okra to lose its "sliminess," one must make slits in each piece of okra. Place in a bowl and cover with water and white wine vinegar. Place in a sunny spot and wait 1 hour. Peel and chop the tomatoes. Rinse the okra.

Place the onion and olive oil in a skillet and allow the onion to sweat and become translucent over a low fire. Add the okra and cook for 5 minutes. Add the tomatoes and parsley, and season with pepper. (This dish needs lots of pepper.)

Let the vegetables stew until the okra is completely tender and most of the liquid has evaporated.

Yield: 6 servings

ROASTED CORN ON THE COB
>KALABOKI TIS SXARAS

INGREDIENTS

12 Ears fresh corn
¼ Cup extra virgin olive oil

When you visit Greece in the summer months, one of the things you see is the street vendor selling roasted corn on the cob. They roast the corn over a charcoal fire right there on the street. The roasting creates a lovely sweetness from the fructose (natural sugar) in the corn.

Shell and remove the outer leaves and the fine corn silk. Preheat the charcoal grill to medium-high heat. Brush the grill with olive oil. Place the ears of corn on the grill and turn them as they roast. They are done when they are golden brown on all sides.

SAUTEED BABY SPINACH WITH FRESH TOMATOES

>TRYFERO SPANAKI TIS CATSAROLAS ME FRESCES TOMATES

INGREDIENTS

1 Small Vidalia onion or other sweet onion, chopped very fine
1 Tablespoon of fresh parsley, chopped very fine
2 Cloves garlic, chopped very fine
1 10.5 Ounce Can low-sodium vegetable broth
3 Tablespoons extra virgin olive oil
6 Roma tomatoes, peeled and chopped very fine
2 Pounds fresh baby spinach
Salt and fresh-ground black pepper to taste

Sauté onions and extra virgin olive oil until soft and translucent. Add garlic and parsley. Sauté 2 minutes, and add tomatoes. Turn fire to high for 5 minutes. Add the vegetable broth. Cover and cook on low flame for 15 minutes. Add spinach and cook 5 minutes over medium fire or until spinach is wilted. Salt and pepper to taste.

SPINACH AND ARTICHOKE CASSEROLE
>SPANAKI AGINARES KATSAROLA

INGREDIENTS

1 Large onion, chopped finely
1 Bunch scallions, chopped finely
1 Tablespoon extra virgin olive oil
5 15 Ounce cans artichoke hearts
(cut half of them in half
and chop the rest)
4 Packages frozen spinach
1½ Cup ricotta cheese
1½ Cup cottage cheese
½ Cup Parmesan cheese
¼ Teaspoon nutmeg
Salt and fresh-ground black
pepper to taste
Breadcrumbs (unseasoned)

Add olive oil to a saucepan and sauté onions and scallions until translucent. Add artichoke hearts for 30 seconds. In a separate pot, boil the spinach and drain it well.

In a large bowl, mix the onions, scallions, and hearts of artichoke with the spinach. Add the ricotta and cottage cheese and half of the Parmesan, Salt and pepper to taste. Add the nutmeg. Mix well. Pour into a ceramic cooking dish. Top with a mixture of the breadcrumbs and Parmesan cheese. Cover with aluminum foil.

Put into a preheated oven at 350 degrees for 25 minutes. Remove the foil and let it get crispy on top (about 10 minutes).

STUFFED GRAPE LEAVES
WITH CHOPPED MEAT
>DOLMATHES ME KIMA

INGREDIENTS

1½ Pounds tender grape leaves
2 Pounds chopped meat
(mixture of veal, pork, and beef)
4 to 6 Bunches scallions, chopped,
or 1½ Pounds onions, chopped
1 Cup extra virgin olive oil
½ Cup raw rice (preferably Uncle
Ben's long-grain rice)
½ Cup chopped fresh parsley
½ Teaspoon chopped fresh mint
2 Eggs, well beaten
Salt and pepper
1 Lemon, juice only
2 Tablespoons butter
Water as needed

Buy the prepared grapevine leaves and wash them in cold water before using.

Mix together the meat, rice, mint, parsley, onions, egg whites, and salt and pepper. Sauté in olive oil until the meat is browned. Allow to cool. Add the eggs and mix well with your hands.

When filling the leaves, keep the shiny side of the leaf on the outside. Put one tablespoon of filling in the center of the leaf and fold the sides up over it, covering it. Roll it like a cigar. Fold the ends under. Lay the stuffed leaves in a pot (open side down so they do not swell open.) in even, tight rows. When one layer is completed, make a second and third layer. Lay a plate directly on top layer of the dolmathes. Add enough water to the pot to half cover the leaves and add butter. Cover the pot. Simmer for about 1 hour until 1½ cups of liquid remain.

Recipe options: Pine nuts or raisins can be added to the stuffing.

Serving options: Usually served cold with lemon wedges. Can also be served hot with avgolemono sauce.

WARM GREENS
>HORTA

INGREDIENTS

Any of the following bitter greens can be used for this dish:
Amaranth (Vlyta)
Dandelion
Swiss Chard
Spinach
Arugula
Chicory
Kale
Collards
Beet Greens

3 Tablespoons extra virgin olive oil
2 Cloves garlic, smashed
2 Pounds fresh, well-washed greens, drained well
Water
2 Tablespoons lemon juice
Salt and fresh-ground black pepper

Horta is served as a side dish with both fish and meat. It is a very healthy everyday dish that is served instead of salad. There are many types of wild greens that are prepared this way:

Place the greens in a large pot of water and bring to a boil. Cook until the greens are wilted and soft. Drain well. In a skillet, sauté the garlic in olive oil. Remove the garlic. Pour the garlic-flavored oil over the greens and toss with the lemon juice. Set aside and serve when the greens reach room temperature.

Chef's trick: This dish needs lots of fresh ground pepper.

Note: Some greens take longer than others to become soft and tender.
The Greeks often save the cooking liquid. It makes a very healthy drink when it is cold.

SEAFOOD

SEAFOOD SELECTION

When you buy fish and shellfish, absolute freshness is essential.

It is best to buy the fish the same day you plan to eat it. Do not keep it more than twenty-four hours, and be sure it is tightly covered in the refrigerator. Look for clear, bright eyes and firm flesh. If there is a slight scent of ammonia, the fish is not fresh.

With shellfish such as mussels and clams, be sure that the shells are tightly closed. Ask the fishmonger to open one. Have him squeeze lemon on the flesh. If it is fresh, it will move a little. Another trick to ensure freshness is to take any that are open and press the shells together lightly. If they don't close, discard them. After you cook shellfish, discard any shells that do not open.

When choosing lobsters or crabs, be sure they are alive and moving about when you buy them. They will usually stay alive for a day in the refrigerator. Be sure to open the bag a bit so they can breathe, but not escape.

FRYING FISH

For the Greeks, frying fish is one of the most traditional and delicious ways to eat some types of fish. It is especially well suited for small fish, such as porgies, whitebait, and sardines. It is also a popular way to cook shrimp.

To evenly coat the fish, place all-purpose flour and cornmeal in a plastic bag with a little salt and pepper. Put the fish in the bag and seal it. Turn the bag over several times. In a deep pot, preheat the oil to 325–375 degrees. The Greeks generally use a light olive oil or corn oil.

CHAR-GRILLED FISH
>PSITO PSARI

FISH USED FOR GRILLING:

Porgy/tsipoura
Fresh sardines/sarthela
Red mullet/barbouni
Sea bass/rofos
Grouper/stira
Red snapper/synagritha
Swordfish/xifias
Tuna/tonnos
Octopus/htapothi
Bronzini/lavraki

In Greece, the most popular method for cooking fish is grilling. Fish is usually grilled whole with the head on. To clean the fish, first remove the scales by using a fish scaler or a sharp knife. Cut the belly open and remove the intestines. Using your index finger, remove the gills. Wash well in cold water and pat dry.

Heat the barbecue. It is important to spray or brush the grill with oil before putting the fish on the grill or it will stick and be hard to turn over.

Brush the fish with a mixture of extra virgin olive oil, lemon juice, and either fresh thyme or oregano. Save a little of this mixture to pour over the fish when it is done.

Serving suggestions: Grilled fish in Greece is typically served with horta (wild greens), boiled potatoes with chopped fresh parsley and lemon wedges.

MEDITERRANEAN BAKED FISH
>PSARI PLAKI

INGREDIENTS

2 Cloves minced garlic
1 Large Spanish onion, minced
1 Medium bunch flat – leaf
parsley, chopped
4 Stalks celery, chopped
1 Large green pepper, chopped
Juice of ½ lemon
1 Cup white wine
1 Lemon slice (seeds removed)
½ Cup breadcrumbs
1 Cup tomato sauce
4 Large red potatoes, peeled and
cut into ½ inch pieces
3 Cups water

Choose any white-meat fish (red snapper, stripe bass, grouper, cod, etc.). Ask your fishmonger to scale and gut the fish but leave the head and tail on. You can also use steaks of large white-meat fish such as halibut, scrod, or swordfish. You will need approximately 4 pounds of fish for 6 people.

Place fish in a large roasting pan (3 inches deep). Score one side of the fish with a sharp knife. Surround the fish with chopped vegetables and herbs. Add tomato sauce, water, and white wine. Sprinkle the top of the fish with breadcrumbs, drizzle with olive oil, and garnish with lemon slices.
Bake fish at 375° for 1 hour.

Serving suggestions: Serve fish in either a deep plate or a large soup bowl. Spoon plenty of the sauce over the fish and serve with fresh hot French or Italian bread for dipping in the sauce.

BAKED FISH WITH TOMATOES AND SCALLIONS
>PSARI SPETSIOTA

INGREDIENTS

4 Pounds of whole fish
1 Teaspoon fresh oregano,
chopped finely
½ Cup fresh breadcrumbs
½ Cup extra virgin olive oil
3 Large fresh tomatoes, sliced thin
1 Bunch scallions,
cleaned and chopped
1 Cup fresh parsley,
chopped coarsely
1 Clove garlic, minced
2 Large sweet onions,
peeled and chopped
2 Lemons, sliced thin
1 Cup water or chicken stock
2 Tablespoons butter
½ Cup dry white wine
Salt and fresh-ground black pepper

Ask your fishmonger to scale and gut the fish. Wash the fish well, inside and out. Remove the gills and the eyes. Striped bass, red snapper, black fish, sea bass, halibut, cod, or haddock are the best fish for this dish.

Preheat the oven to 350 degrees. Place the whole fish in a greased baking pan and sprinkle with salt and pepper, oregano, and olive oil. Add the tomato slices, scallions, parsley, and garlic. Top with fresh bread-crumbs and dot with butter. Garnish with onion rings and lemon slices. Add the water or chicken broth and white wine. Cover the baking dish with aluminum foil and bake the fish for 30 minutes. Remove the foil and turn the oven to 400 degrees. Continue baking for 15 minutes.

Serving suggestion: Plaki is usually served with rice pilaf. The vegetables and the sauce are placed on top of the rice.

Variation: Filets of fish can be used instead of whole fish; however, the skin should be left on. You will need about ½ pound of filets per person.

Chef's trick: To be sure the fish is done, take a fork and push it into the fish until you touch the bone. Move the fork back a bit. If the fish is done, the meat will be white and flaky to the bone. If it is not done, it will still appear to be translucent.

CHAR-GRILLED SARDINES
>PSITES SARDELLES

INGREDIENTS

30 Fresh sardines
4 Tablespoons extra virgin olive oil
Juice of 1 lemon
2 Teaspoons fresh thyme,
chopped

MARINADE:
1 Cup extra virgin olive oil
1 Tablespoon fresh thyme or
oregano, chopped finely
Salt and fresh-ground
pepper to taste

Sardines are blessed with Omega 3 oil and are considered to be heart-healthy.

In Greece, the most popular method for cooking fish is grilling. Fish is usually grilled whole with the head on. To clean the fish, first remove the scales by using a fish scaler or a sharp knife. Cut the belly open and remove the intestines. Using your index finger, remove the gills. Wash well in cold water and pat dry.

Chef's trick: Save a little of this mixture to pour over the fish when it is done.
Marinate the sardines by placing them in a zip lock plastic bag with the marinade for 1 hour. Heat the bar-beque. It is important the spray or brush the grill with oil before putting the fish on the grill or it will stick and be hard to turn over. Place the sardines on the grill for 2 minutes on each side. Remove from the grill and place on paper towels to drain. Plate the sardines and squeeze the juice of a lemon over the fish.

Serving suggestions: These fish are best served with French fries and horta (wild greens).

FRIED SALTED CURED COD
>BAKALIARO TIGHANITO ME SKORDALIA

INGREDIENTS

1 Side of salted cod
1½ Cups flour
½ Teaspoon salt
Pinch of pepper
½ Teaspoon toasted sweet paprika
Water
Corn oil for frying

This dish requires at least 24 hours to prepare.

Soak the cod in a large ceramic bowl of cold water for 24 hours in the refrigerator. Change the water several times. Drain on paper towels and cut into serving-size pieces. In a large zip-lock bag, place the flour, paprika, salt, and pepper. Shake it well. Add the cod and zip the bag. Turn the bag over several times to thoroughly coat the fish. In a large frying pan, put 1 inch of oil, and using a medium heat, bring the oil to temperature for frying. Add the pieces of fish, one at a time. Do not overfill the pan. Drain on paper towels and serve hot with skordalia (see sauces.)

Variations:

1. Greek housewives often make a batter for frying. They mix the flour, salt, and pepper with 1 teaspoon of baking powder and add water until the mixture reaches the consistency of pancake batter. They then dip the fish into the batter and drop it into the hot oil.

2. To make a very crispy fried fish, the Japanese have a product called Panko (toasted breadcrumbs), which can be used instead of the flour, water, and baking powder.

PHYLLIS'S CODFISH CAKES
>KEFTEDES BACALIAROU

INGREDIENTS

**2 Pounds good-quality fresh
codfish filets, de-boned,
or dried codfish that has
been de-salted for 48 hours in
water in the refrigerator
(change the water often)
2 Tablespoons pimiento strips
1 Teaspoon fresh thyme,
chopped finely
3 Eggs
1 Large boiled potato, peeled
1 Teaspoon Worcestershire sauce
2 Tablespoons
chopped flat-leaf parsley
2 Tablespoons butter
3 Tablespoons extra virgin olive
Salt and pepper to taste**

Mix together all of the ingredients except for the olive oil and butter and make into patties. Sauté in the butter and oil over medium fire until they are golden brown.

Serving suggestions:
1 bunch arugula, well washed
1 teaspoon lemon juice
2 tablespoons extra virgin olive oil
Remove the hard stems from the arugula. Dress the arugula and serve cod cakes on top or use fresh greens of your choice.

Or serve with warm tomato sauce.
(see sauces page 220)

SPICY CODFISH WITH TOMATOES AND POTATOES
>PIKANTICOS BACALIAROS ME TOMATES KE PATATES

INGREDIENTS

36 Ounces fresh codfish, cut into 6 Pieces
3 Tablespoons all-purpose flour
5 Medium tomatoes, peeled, seeded, and chopped finely
2 Tablespoons fresh flat-leaf parsley, chopped finely
1 Tablespoon of fresh thyme, chopped finely
4 Cloves garlic, minced finely
4 Large sweet onions
Juice of ½ lemon
¼ Cup celery, chopped coarsely
1 Cup dry white wine
2 Sprigs saffron
1 Cup extra virgin olive oil
6 Large russet potatoes, washed, peeled, and cut into ¼" slices
Red pepper flakes to taste

In a heavy skillet, over a medium fire, brown the potatoes in 1 cup olive oil until brown and crisp, but not completely done. Remove the potatoes and set aside. Throw out the oil. Wipe the skillet clean with a paper towel. Wash the fish in cold water and pat dry with a paper towel. Add salt and pepper to the flour and dredge the fish in flour. Add the remaining olive oil to the same skillet; and over a medium-high fire, fry the fish until golden brown. Set aside on paper towels to drain. Throw out the remaining oil and clean the pan. Add 2 tablespoons of oil to the pan and caramelize the onions and saffron until they are translucent. Add the garlic and cook for 30 seconds. Add ½ cup white wine and allow it to evaporate about 3 minutes. Add the tomatoes, parsley, and thyme and cook over a low fire for 30 minutes. Add the potatoes and mix with the sauce. Place the fish filets on top of the potatoes and sauce. Add ½ cup white wine and bake uncovered in a 400-degree oven for 25 minutes.

Serving suggestion: Serve with fresh crusty bread.

Variation: Add three medium zucchini, peeled and sliced to the frying potatoes.

CHAR-GRILLED CODFISH
>BACALIAROS STA CARVOUNA

INGREDIENTS

6 2-Inch-thick pieces fresh codfish
Cooking wine
½ Cup extra virgin olive oil
**1 Teaspoon fresh thyme,
chopped finely**
**1 Tablespoon fresh flat leaf
parsley, chopped finely**
3 Cloves of garlic, sliced thin
1 Small piece fatback
**Salt and fresh-ground
pepper to taste**

Wash the fish well and salt and pepper the fish steaks. Put the olive oil, thyme, and garlic in a shallow ceramic dish. Tie the fish steaks so they hold together. Put the fish steaks in the marinade for 3 hours. Turn them at least twice. Preheat the charcoal grill so that you have a very hot fire.

Rub the grill with the fatback to keep the fish from sticking. Place the fish steaks on the grill (reserve the garlic and oil) and allow them to caramelize on one side for 5 minutes. Use a wide spatula to turn them. Caramelize them on the other side. Serve them hot with a teaspoon of the marinade drizzled over them. Sprinkle them with the parsley.

Serving suggestions: This dish is served with a horta salad.

GRILLED TUNA WITH TOMATO GARNISH
>TONOS TIS SHARAS ME TOMATES

INGREDIENTS

**3 Pounds fresh tuna, cut into
slices no thicker than ½ inch**
4 Tablespoons extra virgin olive oil
**6 Small tomatoes, stems
removed, diced fine**
3 Tablespoons large Greek capers
Balsamic vinegar to taste
**2 Bunches baby arugula,
washed well**
Freshly ground pepper to taste

Brush the tuna slices lightly with olive oil. Grill on a hot, oiled outdoor grill or in a preheated hot broiler for about 5 minutes, turning once. Do not overcook; the fish will continue to cook for 1 or 2 minutes even after you remove it from the grill. Remove the fish to a platter to cool. To make the garnish, mix the tomatoes, capers, olive oil, and vinegar in a small bowl. Before serving, line individual plates with a bed of the arugula. Place the grilled tuna on the arugula and garnish with 2 tablespoons or so of the tomato mixture. Grind black pepper over the top of each dish.

CLAMS STEAMED IN WHITE WINE
>AXIVATHES ME ASPRO KRASI

INGREDIENTS

6 Pounds small clams
2 Cups dry white wine
1/3 Cup extra virgin olive oil
6 Cloves garlic
1 Cup fresh flat-leaf parsley,
chopped finely
4 Teaspoons butter

Scrub the clams under cold running water to remove any sand. Place them in a large pot with the white wine and a cup of water. Steam over medium-high heat covered until the clams open, about 4 minutes. Drain in a colander. Reserve the liquid.

In the same pot, heat the olive oil over a medium fire. Add the garlic and the parsley. Add in the reserved white wine (be sure to strain it though cheesecloth to avoid any grit). Toss in the butter and the clams. Remove from heat.

Serving suggestions: Serve in large bowls with fresh crusty bread. Always put a dish nearby for the shells.

STUFFED CLAMS
>GEMISTES AXIVATHES

INGREDIENTS

36 Washed Little Neck or
Cherrystone clams
4 Slices bacon
Breadcrumbs (unseasoned)
2 Tablespoons fresh flat-leaf
parsley, chopped
1 Teaspoon fresh thyme,
chopped finely
2 Cloves garlic, minced
1 Cup dry white wine

Place the clams in a bowl of cold water and wash the outside of the shells with a small brush to remove any sand. You may need to wash them more than once. Open the clams and reserve the juice. Using a clam knife, release the muscle so the clams are easy to remove from the shell. Place the open clams in a baking dish. Make a mixture of the breadcrumbs, garlic, parsley, and thyme. Lightly sprinkle each clam with the breadcrumb mixture. Put a small piece of bacon on top of each clam. Pour 1 cup white wine and the juice of the clams in the bottom of the baking dish; broil for 20 minutes or until the bacon is done.

BOILED SHRIMP
>VRASTES GARIDES

INGREDIENTS

36 Medium to large shrimp, shell on
½ Cup extra virgin olive oil
½ Lemon
2 Tablespoon fresh parsley,
chopped finely
Juice of ½ lemon
1 Rib celery, cut into 2-inch pieces
Salt and fresh-ground black
pepper to taste

Bring a large saucepan of water to a rolling boil. Add the celery and the shrimp. When to water comes back to a boil, turn off the heat and cover tightly for 5 minutes. Remove the shrimp and immerse in an ice bath. Peel, shell, and devein the shrimp. Whisk together the olive oil and lemon juice. Pour the dressing over the shrimp and sprinkle to top with parsley, salt, and pepper.

Serving suggestion: This dish can be served as an appetizer or as a main course with the dilled English peas.

CHAR-GRILLED SHRIMP
>PSITES GARIDES

INGREDIENTS

18 Medium shrimp
(3 per person)

MARINADE:
2 Tablespoons fennel fronds,
chopped finely
1 Tablespoon fresh parsley,
chopped finely
2 Tablespoons fresh thyme,
chopped finely
1 Cup extra virgin olive oil
Juice of 1 lemon

Clean and remove the shell. Using a small paring knife, cut down the top of the shrimp and remove the intestinal tract. Wash the shrimp well in cold water. Place a paper towel in the bottom of a large strainer. Put the shrimp in the strainer to drain for 15 minutes. Remove and pat dry. Put the shrimp a plastic zip-lock bag. Add the marinade. Put in the refrigerator for 30 minutes.
Remove and place on a very hot grill for 1½ to 2 minutes per side. If you cook it too long, it will become tough. When it turns pink, it is done.

Serving suggestions: This dish can either be served over rice as a main course or with Mediterranean salad as an appetizer.

Variations: Fresh basil can be substituted for the fennel.

SHRIMPS WITH FETA AND TOMATOES
>GARIDES A LA GREQUE

INGREDIENTS

**36 Medium to large shrimp,
cleaned and deveined
1 Tablespoon shallots, minced
2 Cloves garlic, minced
1 Medium onion, minced
Salt and pepper
1 Tablespoon fresh thyme
(or dried oregano)
4 Medium tomatoes, peeled,
seeded, and chopped
1 Tablespoon fresh flat-leaf
parsley, chopped finely
1 Cup dry white wine
3 Tablespoons extra virgin olive oil
¼ Pound crumbled feta cheese**

In a large frying pan, over a hot fire, sauté the shrimp in olive oil until they are opaque. Remove and set aside. Sauté the shallots and onion for 5 minutes. Add the garlic and thyme. Sauté 1 minute; add the wine and allow it to evaporate for 1 minute. Add the tomatoes. Cover and simmer for 10 minutes. Add the shrimp and place the pan under the broiler for 5 minutes. Add the Feta and continue under the broiler for 3 minutes. Finish the dish by sprinkling the finely chopped parsley over the top.

Serving Suggestion: Serve over rice.

SHRIMP WITH PEPPERS
>GARIDES ME PIPERIES

INGREDIENTS

**3 Cups cooked shrimp,
peeled and deveined
2 Tablespoons extra virgin olive oil
2 Medium onions, chopped
½ Red bell pepper, diced
½ Yellow bell pepper, diced
1½ Cups celery, diced
12 Medium tomatoes,
seeded and diced
2 Tablespoons tomato paste
Salt and pepper to taste
1 Teaspoon sugar
2 Strips bacon, rendered**

In a large skillet, sauté the onions, celery, and peppers in bacon drippings and olive oil until the onions are translucent, about 15 minutes. Add the tomatoes, tomato paste, and sugar. Let the mixture simmer slowly until the sauce is thick, 30–45 minutes on a low fire. Add salt and pepper. Add the shrimp and cook for 10 minutes. Note: the sauce can be made a day ahead.

Variation: Add ½ cup of crumbled Feta cheese at the same time as the shrimp and cook in a preheated oven at 400 degrees for 10 minutes.

Serving suggestion: Typically this dish is served over orzo or rice.

MUSSELS STEAMED IN WHITE WINE
>MIDIA ME ASPRO KRASI

INGREDIENTS

6 Pounds mussels
2 Cups dry white wine
1/3 Cup extra virgin olive oil
6 Cloves of garlic
1 Cup fresh flat-leaf parsley,
chopped finely
4 Teaspoons butter

Scrub the mussels under cold running water. Pull off the tough beards. Place mussels in a large pot with the white wine and a cup of water and steam over a medium-high heat covered until the mussels open, about 4 minutes. Drain in a colander. Reserve the liquid.

In the same pot, heat the olive oil over a medium fire. Add the garlic and the parsley. Add in the reserved white wine (be sure to strain it though cheesecloth to avoid any grit). Toss in the butter and the mussels. Remove from the heat.

Serving suggestions: Serve in large bowls with fresh crusty bread. Always put a dish nearby for the shells.

FRIED SQUID
>KALAMARI

INGREDIENTS

3 Pounds baby squid
1 Cup all-purpose flour
2 Tablespoons corn meal
1 Cup fresh flat-leaf parsley,
chopped finely
2 Tablespoons lemon zest
½ Teaspoon salt
Extra virgin olive oil or vegetable
oil for frying
2 Lemons

Wash and clean the squid. Remove the ink sacs. Cut the bodies into rings and remove and reserve the tentacles. On paper towels, dry the squid well. In a large plastic zip-lock bag, mix the salt, lemon zest, flour, corn meal, and cayenne pepper well. Put the squid in the bag. Zip it well and turn it upside down several times or until all the squid is well coated. In a large frying pan, place enough oil for frying, about ½ inch in depth. Put the pan over a medium-high heat. Fry the squid until golden brown on one side, about 30 seconds. Turn the squid and remove from the pan when both sides are golden. Drain the squid well on paper towels.

Chef's trick: If you cook the squid too long, it will become tough. Test a piece for doneness before you finish cooking it.

Serving suggestions: This dish can be served as a main course or as appetizer. Garnish the Kalamari with lemon wedges and a dusting of fresh-chopped parsley.

CHAR-GRILLED CALAMARI
>PSITO KALAMARI

INGREDIENTS

18 Medium calamari
(3 per person)

MARINADE:
2 Tablespoons fennel fronds,
chopped finely
1 Tablespoon fresh parsley
2 Tablespoons fresh Thyme
1 Cup extra virgin olive oil
Juice of 1 lemon

Clean and remove the thin bone inside the calamari. Wash the calamari well in cold water. Place a paper towel in the bottom of a large strainer. Put the calamari in the strainer to drain for 15 minutes. Remove and pat dry. Put the calamari a plastic zip-lock bag. Add the marinade. Put in the refrigerator for 1–2 hours.
Remove and place on a very hot grill for 1½ to 2 minutes per side. If you cook it too long, it will become tough.

Serving suggestions: This dish can either be served over rice as a main course or with Mediterranean salad as an appetizer.

Variation: Fresh basil can be substituted for the fennel.

STUFFED CALAMARI
>KALAMARAKIA GEMISTA

INGREDIENTS

20 Medium calamari
¼ Cup toasted pine nuts
¼ Cup yellow raisins
½ Red wine
1 Teaspoon tomato paste
¼ Cup fresh flat-leaf parsley,
chopped finely
2 Small shallots, peeled and
chopped finely
1 Bay leaf
1 Tablespoon unsalted butter
1 Tablespoon extra virgin olive oil
1 Bay leaf
1 10.5 Ounce can low-fat, low-
sodium chicken broth
1 Cup long- grain rice (Uncle Ben's)
Water

In a medium saucepan, sauté the shallots and bay leaf in butter and olive oil for 1 minute. Add the rice, pine nuts, and raisins; toast, stirring constantly, for 2 minutes. Dissolve the tomato paste in the red wine; add to pan. Add chicken broth and water as needed. Bring to a rolling boil and cook uncovered until most of the liquid is reduced to the same height in the pot as the rice. Cover tightly and remove from the stove. Do not allow the rice to completely cook, as it will cook some more inside the calamari.
Preheat oven to 350 degrees.

When the rice is cool enough to work with, add the fresh parsley; stuff the calamari with the rice mixture. Close each one with a toothpick. Lay them side-by-side in a large baking dish. Do not overlap. Pour fresh tomato sauce (refer to the recipe for fresh tomato sauce.) over the top; bake for 45 minutes.

Chef's trick: In order to determine the amount of liquid required to cook the rice, add the chicken broth, then a can of water. You may need to add more water. The liquid needs to be two fingers above the rice before you start it boiling.

SPICY CALAMARI STEW WITH PAPPARDELLE
>PICANTICO KALAMARI ME PAPPARDELLE

INGREDIENTS

**3 Pounds calamari
(both tentacles and body)
Preserve two of the ink sacs
3 Tablespoons extra virgin olive oil
2 Bunches scallions,
chopped finely
3 Tablespoons fresh flat-leaf
parsley, chopped finely
3 Stalks celery, chopped finely
3 Large cloves garlic,
minced finely
½ Cup white wine
2 Cups water
2 Medium tomatoes,
chopped finely
1 Teaspoon tomato paste
12 Kalamata olives,
pitted and rinsed well
½ Teaspoon red pepper flakes
Salt and pepper to taste
1 Pound pappardelle**

Sauté the squid in olive oil for two minutes, or until it turns red. Add everything else except the wine. Cook over a medium fire for 3 minutes, stirring constantly. Add the wine and cook for one minute or until it evaporates. Add tomatoes, tomato paste, red pepper flakes, and two cups of water. Cover tightly and cook over a low to medium fire for 1 hour. Add the olives and cook for five more minutes.

Bring 4 quarts of water to a boil. Add ½ teaspoon sea salt and the ink. Add the pappardelle and cook 8 to 10 minutes, or until the pasta is al dente.

Serving suggestions: Serve the spicy squid over pappardelle with good-quality crusty bread.

BAKED STUFFED LOBSTER
>GEMISTI ASTAKI

INGREDIENTS

**6 Lobsters, 1½ to 2 pounds each
(ask for the hard-shelled lobsters)
6 Cups fresh breadcrumbs
4 Cloves of garlic, finely minced
2 Tablespoons sweet onion,
chopped finely
1 Teaspoon fresh mint,
chopped finely
3 Tablespoons fresh parsley,
chopped finely
1 Tablespoon fresh thyme,
chopped finely
3 Tablespoons extra virgin olive oil
3 Tablespoons clarified butter (ghee)
1 Tablespoontablespoons sweet
toasted paprika
½ Cup ice water**

Using a lobster pot or a very large stockpot, bring 6 quarts of water to a boil. Drop the lobsters into the boiling water, headfirst. Bring the water back to a boil and cook the lobsters for 10 minutes. Do not overcook them, because they will cook again in another step. Remove the lobsters from the pot and set them aside to cool for 10 minutes. Place the lobsters on baking sheets and preheat the oven to 350 degrees. Roll each lobster on its back. Using a very sharp, strong chef's knife, split the belly from the head to the tip of the tail. Do not cut all the way through. Remove the green mass from the head. In a large mixing bowl, mix together the breadcrumbs, garlic, onion, mint, parsley, thyme, and olive oil. Add ¼ cup of ice water and mix well.

Stuff the cavity of each lobster with the mixture. Sprinkle each lobster with paprika and drizzle with the clarified butter.

Bake the lobsters for 15 to 20 minutes or until the stuffing is nicely browned.

Serving suggestions: Garnish with lemon wedges and fresh parsley and serve with roasted corn on the cob.

Chef's trick: Adding ice water to the stuffing will help keep it light.

SEPIA CUTTLEFISH WITH RICE AND SPINACH
>SOUPIA ME RIZI KE SPANAKI

INGREDIENTS

**3 Pounds sepia,
both tentacles and body
(Preserve two ink sacs when you
clean the sepia.)
3 Tablespoons extra virgin olive oil
2 Bunches scallions,
chopped finely
3 Tablespoons fresh parsley,
chopped finely
3 Stalks celery, chopped finely
2 Cups fresh spinach, chopped
3 Large cloves garlic,
chopped finely
½ Cup white wine
Juice of ¼ lemon
2 Cups water
Salt and pepper
1 Pound raw long grain rice**

To clean the sepia, remove the long flat bone and remove the ink sacs. Wash well.

Sauté the sepia in olive oil for two minutes until it turns red. Add everything else except the wine. Cook over medium heat for 3 minutes, stirring constantly. Add the wine and cook for one minute or until it evaporates. Add two cups of water and the ink. Cover tightly and cook over low to medium heat for 1 hour. Add the rice. (Make sure there is enough liquid.) Cover the pot and cook for 20 minutes or until all the liquid is absorbed. Five minutes before you finish cooking it, add in the chopped fresh spinach. Squeeze the juice of ¼ of a lemon over the top.

Serving suggestion: Serve with a French baguette or other crusty bread.

CRAB CAKES
>CAVOURO KEFTEDES

INGREDIENTS

2 Pounds good-quality fresh or pasteurized crabmeat
2 Tablespoons pimiento strips
1 Teaspoon fresh thyme
3 Eggs
¼ Cup freshly made breadcrumbs
1 Teaspoon Worcestershire sauce
2 Tablespoons chopped flat leaf parsley
2 Tablespoons butter
3 Tablespoons extra virgin olive
Salt and pepper to taste

Mix together all of the ingredients except for the olive oil and butter and make into patties. Sauté in the butter and oil over medium fire until they are golden brown.

Serving suggestion:
1 bunch arugula, well washed
1 teaspoon lemon juice
2 tablespoons extra virgin olive oil
Remove the hard stems from the arugula. Dress the arugula and serve crab cakes on top or use fresh greens of your choice.

SEVEN ISLAND MEDITERRANEAN SEAFOOD STEW
>KAKAVIA

INGREDIENTS

1 Cup roasted tomatoes, peeled
4 Tablespoons extra virgin olive oil
1 Cup white wine
1 Tablespoon tomato paste
1 Tablespoon all-purpose flour
2 Handfuls fresh flat-leaf parsley, chopped finely
½ Red pepper, chopped finely
½ Cup celery, chopped finely
1/3 Cup carrots, chopped finely
1/3 Medium onion, chopped finely
1 Tablespoon garlic, minced finely
3 Medium potatoes, peeled and cubed
2 Cups low-sodium chicken broth
3 Cups water
2 Dozen small clams
2 Dozen mussels
1 1¼ Pound lobster
1 Pound shrimp
1 Pound firm white fish, cut into 2-Inch strips

Wash the tomatoes well and cut the tops off. Place them in a roasting pan and sprinkle them with sea salt. Let them stand for about 1 hour. Roast them in the oven at 350 degrees until the edges are lightly blackened. Remove them and let them cool. Remove the skin. In a large pot, caramelize celery, carrots, onion, and pepper in extra virgin olive oil. Add garlic. Add 1 cup white wine and let it cook for 2-3 minutes. Add roasted tomatoes, tomato paste and flour. Stir well.

Add chicken broth and water. Bring to a boil and add potatoes. Cook seven minutes. Add parsley. Add the shellfish and cook for 5 minutes. Lower the fire and add the fish. Cook with the lid on for 5 minutes. Serves six.

Serving Suggestion: Serve with slices of toasted country bread topped with a dollop of Garlic Aioli Sauce. (see sauces page 224)

MEATS

KREAS

TRADITIONAL LEG OF LAMB
>PSITO BOUTI ARNIOU

INGREDIENTS

**1 Leg of young spring lamb
(not frozen)
3–4 Cloves of garlic
Salt and pepper
1 Tablespoon fresh thyme,
chopped finely
1 Tablespoon fresh rosemary,
chopped finely
4 Tablespoons extra virgin olive oil
Juice of one lemon
2 Cups hot water**

Wash the leg of lamb in cold water and pat dry. With a sharp paring knife, make small slits about 2 inches a part all over the meat. Thinly slice the garlic. Mix together the thyme, salt, and pepper in a separate small bowl. Put a little of the seasoning mixture and a sliver of garlic in each of the slits in the lamb. Be sure to do both sides of the lamb. Brush the lamb with the olive oil and lemon juice mixture.

Preheat the oven to 450 degrees. Cook in a roasting pan, fat side up. Place the roast in the oven for 30 minutes. Reduce the heat to 350 degrees and add the water. Traditionally, Greeks like their lamb well done (170f). For medium lamb, the internal temperature should be 150 to 160 degrees. You may need to add water. Remove the lamb and let it rest while deglazing the pan drippings. Serve the lamb with the juices.

Chef's tricks: The chef should always smell the lamb in the butcher shop. If the lamb has a strong smell, it is not a spring lamb; the cooked roast may have a strong mutton taste.

WHOLE BABY SPRING LAMB ON THE SPIT
>ARNAKI TIS SOUVLAS

MARINADE:

2 Cups extra virgin olive oil
4 Cloves garlic, smashed
1 Tablespoon oregano
Salt and pepper to taste

Note: You can use a mixture of olive oil and Fytini (margarine) or melted butter.

On Greek Easter, the aroma of lamb cooking over charcoal permeates the air. Fresh baby lamb is only available in the spring. If a lamb weighs more than 30 pounds, it is considered a sign that it is too old.

In modern times, you can purchase an outdoor wood-fired grill especially designed for cooking a whole lamb or pig. It comes with a motorized rotisserie. Most of the large Greek markets carry them.

A few weeks before you need it, ask your butcher to get a 25- to 30-pound lamb with the head on. Have him remove the innards and reserve the liver. The liver is cooked separately on skewers with bacon and onion.

Note: A 25-pound lamb will serve about 25 people.

First the spear for the rotisserie is inserted and the clamps provided with the grill are tightened down well to hold the lamb in place. You don't want the lamb to twist on the spit. Tie the front and back legs together. The inside of the lamb is rubbed with sprigs of thyme, oregano, salt, and pepper. Small slits are cut into the inside of the belly and slivers of garlic are inserted. The thyme sprigs are sewn inside the belly using a surgical needle and butcher's twine.

When the charcoal turns red and the fire dies down, put the spit in the holders and tighten the clamps. Turn on the rotisserie and roast the lamb for about 6 hours. You will need to baste it with the marinade about every 15 to 20 minutes.

LAMB PATTIES
>KEFTEDES

INGREDIENTS

3 Pounds ground lamb shoulder
1 Large sweet onion,
chopped finely
1 Teaspoon sea salt
2 Tablespoon fresh mint,
chopped finely
2 Tablespoons fresh parsley,
chopped finely
1 Tablespoon dried oregano
(or 2 Tablespoons fresh oregano),
chopped finely
2 Cloves garlic, minced
2 Large eggs

Peel and grate the onion. In a large bowl, use your hands to mix all of the ingredients very well. Refrigerate for 3 to 4 hours. Remove and shape the mixture into oblong patties about the size of a woman's hand. On a preheated and very hot grill, sear the outsides well. Reduce the heat to medium and continue grilling until the meat is done (160f) medium-well.

Chef's trick: Wear surgical gloves when working with raw onions to prevent tears. You can also wash your hands in cold water frequently to reduce tears.

Variations: This dish can be done with beef.
Serving Suggestions: Serve with rice and a traditional Greek salad.

ROAST LEG OF LAMB WITH POTATOES
>ARNI PSITO ME PATATES

INGREDIENTS

1 Leg of young spring lamb
(not frozen)
3–4 Cloves garlic
Salt and pepper
1 Tablespoon fresh thyme,
chopped finely
1 Tablespoon fresh rosemary,
chopped finely
4 Tablespoons extra virgin olive oil
¼ Stick butter
Juice of one lemon
20 Small potatoes, peeled
2 Cups hot water

Wash the leg of lamb in cold water and pat dry. With a sharp paring knife, make small slits all over the lamb. Thinly slice the garlic. Mix together the thyme, salt, and pepper in a separate small bowl. Put a little of the mixture and a sliver of garlic in each of the slits in the lamb. Be sure to do both sides of the lamb. Brush the lamb with the olive oil and lemon juice mixture.

Preheat the oven to 450 degrees. Cook in a roasting pan, fat side up. Place the roast in the oven for 30 minutes. Rub the potatoes with salt and pepper and add to the baking pan. Sprinkle the potatoes with small pats of butter. Reduce the heat to 350 degrees and add the water. Traditionally, Greeks like their lamb well done. For medium lamb, the internal temperature should be 150 to 160 degrees. You may need to add water. Remove the lamb and let it rest while de-fatting the pan drippings. Increase the oven temperature to 425 and brown the potatoes for 20 minutes. Serve the lamb with the juices.

Chef's tricks: The chef should always smell the lamb in the butcher shop. If the lamb has a strong smell, it is not a spring lamb; the cooked roast may have a strong mutton taste.

ROAST LAMB WITH ARTICHOKES
>ARNI PSITO ME ANGINARES

INGREDIENTS

1 Leg of Lamb
3–4 Cloves garlic
Salt and pepper
1 Tablespoon fresh oregano,
chopped finely
1 Tablespoon rosemary,
chopped finely
4 Tablespoons extra virgin olive oil
Juice of 6 lemons
2 Cups hot water
6 Young artichokes

Remove the tough outer leaves of the artichokes and trim the bottom of the stems. Cut 1" off the remaining leaves. Rub the artichokes with lemon juice and cut them in half lengthwise. Scrape the choke (fuzzy part) out of the hearts. Place the artichokes in cold salted water with the juice of 2 lemons. This will keep them from turning dark.

Preheat the oven to 450 degrees. Wash the leg of lamb in cold water and pat dry. With a sharp paring knife, make slits in various places. Thinly slice the garlic. Mix together the oregano, salt, and pepper in a separate small bowl. Put a little of the mixture and a sliver of garlic in each of the slits in the lamb. Be sure to do slits on both sides of the lamb. Brush the lamb with the olive oil and lemon juice mixture. Sprinkle with rosemary.

Cook in a roasting pan, fat side up. Place the roast in the oven for 30 minutes. Reduce the heat to 350 degrees and add the water.

Traditionally, Greeks like their lamb well done (170f). For medium lamb, the internal temperature should be 150 to 160 degrees. You may need to add water if the level in the pan gets too low for the meat to stay moist. Remove the lamb and let it rest while de-fatting the pan drippings.

Put the artichokes in the pan with the juices and bake the artichokes, cut side down, for 1 hour (or until tender). You will need to baste them with the pan drippings.

Chef's trick: The chef should always smell the lamb in the butcher shop. If it has a strong smell, it is not fresh.

BRAISED LAMB SHANKS
>PODARAKIA ARNIOU KATSAROLAS

INGREDIENTS

6 Lamb shanks (ask for young lamb)
4 Carrots, cut into 2 inch pieces
4 Stalks celery,
cut into 4 pieces each
1 Large onion, cut into 6 pieces
1 10.5 Ounce can chicken broth
1 10.5 Ounce can beef broth
1 Cup white wine
2 Shallots, chopped finely
2-3 Cloves garlic
2 Tablespoons flour
Water
4 Sprigs thyme
1 Sprig rosemary
2 Tablespoons extra virgin olive oil
2 Tablespoons ghee (clarified butter)

Brown the lamb shanks in olive oil. Set aside. Pour off excess oil, and add ghee. Brown the carrots, celery, shallots, garlic, and onion. Turn off the heat; sprinkle the flour over the vegetables. Stir over a moderate heat until the flour forms a roux that is light brown. Add the white wine and continue stirring until the wine evaporates. Add the thyme, rosemary, beef and chicken broth. Remove the vegetables with a slotted spoon. Put the lamb shanks into the pot and add water just to cover the lamb shanks. Put a tight lid on the pot and put into a 350-degree oven for 1½ to 1¾ hours. Check after 1 hour to be sure there is enough liquid and the shanks are not sticking.

Serving suggestions: This dish is best served with couscous or pasta.

LAMB WITH PEAS
>ARNI ME BIZELIA

INGREDIENTS

3 Pounds of cubed lamb from the leg
3 Tablespoons extra virgin olive oil
1 Tablespoon all-purpose flour
6 Medium tomatoes, diced finely
1 Large onion, chopped finely
1 Clove of garlic, chopped finely
1 Glass dry white wine
**2 Tablespoons fresh parsley,
chopped finely**
3 Cups water
**2 Pounds of fresh, shelled English
peas or frozen peas**

Brown the meat in 2 tablespoons of olive oil. Reserve the meat and pour off all but 1 tablespoon of the oil. Add the other tablespoon of olive oil; sauté the onions until translucent. Add the garlic and cook for 30 seconds. Add one tablespoon of flour and mix. Return the meat to the pot and add the wine, and tomato, and 1 tablespoon parsley. Add the water. Cook over a medium fire for 1 hour, add the peas and continue cooking for 15 minutes.

STUFFED RACK OF LAMB
>GEMISTA PAIDAKIA ARNISIA

INGREDIENTS

2 Racks of baby lamb chops
½ Cup dry white wine
1 Tablespoon extra virgin olive oil

STUFFING:
**2 Tablespoons fresh parsley,
chopped finely**
**1 Teaspoon fresh mint,
chopped finely**
1 Cup breadcrumbs
2 Large cloves garlic, minced finely
1 Tablespoon extra virgin olive oil
2 Egg whites
Salt and pepper

Trim the fat from the racks of lamb and "French" them (directions below). Dust with salt and pepper. In a cast iron skillet, brown the racks of lamb in 1 tablespoon extra virgin olive oil for about 2 minutes on each side. Remove the meat and add the white wine.

To make the stuffing, combine all of the ingredients in a medium bowl and add the whites of two eggs. Mix well. Using your hands, coat the racks with the stuffing. Place the racks in the skillet in a 400-degree oven for 20 minutes for medium rare.

Chef's trick: To "French" the racks, use a sharp paring knife to remove the fat and meat between each rib. Go down one side of the rib, turn the knife, and come back up the other side. Only cut down to the top of the round part of the meat.

LAMB WITH STRING BEANS
>ARNI ME FRESCA FASOULIA

INGREDIENTS

3 Pounds cubed lamb from the leg
3 Tablespoons extra virgin olive oil
1 Tablespoon all-purpose flour
6 Medium-sized tomatoes, diced finely
1 Large onion, chopped finely
1 Clove garlic, chopped finely
1 Glass dry white wine
2 Tablespoons fresh parsley, chopped finely
3 Cups water
2 Pounds fresh or frozen string beans, with the tips cut off

Brown the meat in 2 tablespoons of olive oil. Reserve the meat and pour off all but 1 tablespoon of the oil. Add the other tablespoon of olive oil and sauté the onions until translucent. Add the garlic and cook for 30 seconds. Add one tablespoon of flour; mix. Return the meat to the pot and add the wine, tomato, and 1 tablespoon parsley. Add the water. Cook over a medium fire for 1 hour. Add the string beans and continue cooking for 20 minutes.

LAMB FRICASSEE
>ARNI SOFRITO

INGREDIENTS

**2 Racks of lamb or 8 shoulder
chops (ask the butcher
to remove excess fat)
4 Stalks celery, cut in 2-inch pieces
4 Medium potatoes, peeled and
cut into 2-inch pieces
4 Carrots, scraped and cut into
2-Inch pieces
2 Bunches scallions, chopped
3 Cloves garlic, chopped finely
Juice of ½ lemon
2 Leeks, chopped (be sure to
wash well and only use
the tender green potion)
1 Tablespoon fresh parsley,
chopped finely
2 Tablespoons extra virgin olive oil
1½ Tablespoons flour
2 Tablespoons dill, chopped finely
½ Cup dry white wine
1 Cup chicken broth**

Season the chops with salt and pepper, and brown in extra virgin olive oil. Remove the chops and set aside. Add celery, scallions, garlic, leeks, and parsley. Cook until the ingredients are wilted. Add the lemon juice. Add the flour to make a roux. Do not let the roux brown. Add the wine and the chops; reduce. Add the chicken broth, potatoes, carrots, and 2 cups of water. Cook ½ hour or until the potatoes and carrots are done.
Serves 4.

RACK OF BABY LAMB WITH ORZO
>PAIDAKIA ARNIOU YIOUVETSI

INGREDIENTS

**3 Racks of fresh baby lamb
2 Medium spring onions (remove
the green part and the outer
layers of the onion).
Chop coarsely.
½ Cup dry white wine
1 Tablespoon fresh thyme,
chopped finely
1 Tablespoon fresh flat-leaf
parsley, chopped finely
1 Cup tomato sauce
2 Cloves of garlic, smashed
1 Stalk celery, cut into 2-inch pieces
2 Tablespoons extra virgin olive oil
1 Package orzo (1½ cups)
½ Cup grated Kefalotyri or
Parmesan cheese
Water as needed**

This dish is traditionally made in the spring when the lambs are still less than 30 pounds.

Cut the racks apart, 2 chops at a time. In a large ovenproof pot, brown the chops in olive oil. Remove the chops and set them aside. In the same pan, caramelize the onions, thyme, parsley, garlic, and celery. When the onion is translucent, add the wine and let it evaporate of 1 minute. Add the tomato sauce and cook for 20 minutes. Remove the pot from the heat and strain the sauce. Place the chops and the orzo in the sauce. In a preheated oven, bake the dish until most of the sauce is absorbed. Sprinkle the top with the grated cheese and return it to the oven. Cook until the cheese melts (about 5 minutes).

Note: If you have a good-quality clay pot with a lid, you can bake the yiovetsi in clay, which is the traditional Greek way of doing it.

PROHIBITION LAMB OR LAMB COOKED IN A BROWN BAG
>ARNI KLEFTICO

INGREDIENTS

1 Leg of baby, spring lamb (approximately 5 lbs).
4 Large cloves garlic, cut into slivers
4 Medium carrots, peeled and roughly chopped
2 lbs. Yukon Gold potatoes, peeled and quartered
2 Stalks celery, cut into 2-inch-thick pieces
2 Sprigs fresh thyme
Salt and pepper to taste
2 Tablespoons of Fytini (margarine), softened
1 Brown grocery bag without printing on it

On the leg of lamb, make about 15 slits with a paring knife. Cut 2 cloves of garlic into small pieces, and insert garlic slivers, salt, and pepper into small slits you cut all over the lamb. Rub the lamb with 1 tablespoon of Fytini. Put lamb into brown bag and add the rest of the ingredients to the bag. Close brown bag and tie loosely with string. Put it into a roasting pan and bake in oven at 350° for 1 hour 45 minutes.

Chef's trick: The moisture from the lamb will keep the brown bag from burning.

SKEWERED LAMB'S LIVER
>SIKOTI APO ARNI SOUVLAKI

INGREDIENTS

2 Pounds baby lamb's liver, cut in 2-Inch pieces
10 Strips bacon
2 Medium onions, peeled and cut into eight pieces each

MARINADE:

2 Tablespoons fresh oregano, chopped
4 Cloves garlic, minced
1 Cup extra virgin olive oil
Juice of 1 whole lemon
Salt and pepper

Mix the marinade ingredients together with a wire whisk and pour over the liver pieces. Refrigerate for at least 2 hours. Use either steel or wooden skewers. Start at the very end of the skewer; alternate one piece of liver, one piece of bacon, and one piece of onion. Make sure the meat covers the tip. When your skewer is almost filled, cover the end with aluminum foil. When the skewers are ready, put them on a medium to hot grill for about 8 minutes on each side. Baste them once while they are cooking.

Chef's trick: If you are using wooden skewers, soak them for 2 hours in cold water to keep them from burning on the grill.

MARINATED LAMB'S LIVER AND SAUSAGE
>SICOTI ARNIOU ME LOUKANIKA

INGREDIENTS

**12 Ounces fresh lamb's liver,
cut into cubes
12 Ounces of loukanika (sausage),
cut into 2-inch pieces
1 Medium onion,
cut into 6 wedges**

MARINADE:
**2 Tablespoons extra virgin olive oil
3 Cloves garlic
1 Teaspoon fresh oregano (or
fresh thyme), chopped finely
½ Teaspoon salt
¼ Teaspoon freshly
ground pepper
1 Lemon, cut into wedges**

In a large zip-lock bag, place the marinade, the onion, and the liver. Zip it and refrigerate for at least one hour. Turn it once or twice. Using metal skewers, thread the lamb, onion, and sausage on the skewers. Brush a pre-heated grill with olive oil and place each skewer on the grill. Turn them frequently to keep them from burning.

Chef's trick: If you are using wooden skewers, soak them for 2 hours in cold water to keep them from burning on the grill.

Serving Suggestions: This dish can be served over rice or as a meze.

KEFALONIAN MEAT PIE
>KEFALONITIKI KREATOPITA

INGREDIENTS

6 Pounds lamb, cubed
2/3 Cup extra virgin olive oil
½ Cup red wine
Salt and pepper
1 Tablespoon tomato paste
1 Cup yellow rice
2 Medium onions, chopped finely
5 to 6 Cloves garlic, chopped finely
1 Tablespoon fresh mint, chopped finely
1 Tablespoon fresh oregano, chopped finely
1 Tablespoon fresh dill, chopped finely
2 Tablespoons fresh flat leaf parsley, chopped finely
1 Package of phyllo dough
¼ Pound of unsalted butter, melted
Water

Sauté the onions until they are translucent. Add the garlic and cook for 1 minute. In a separate skillet, brown the meat. When the meat is brown, combine with the onions, garlic, and tomato paste; add the red wine. Cook 3 minutes or until the wine has evaporated. Add the salt, pepper, and herbs and bring to a boil on top of the stove. Boil until the meat is very well done, approximately 1½ hours. Add water as needed. There needs to be some liquid left. Add the rice and turn off the heat. Cover the pot.

Thaw the phyllo dough and keep covered with a damp cloth.

Preheat the oven to 350 degrees.

Oil the bottom of the baking dish. Put in 3 sheets of phyllo, one sheet at a time. Brush melted butter on each sheet. Allow the sheets to extend over the sides. Add the meat mixture and cover it with 3 sheets of phyllo. Fold over the bottom sheets to seal. Brush with butter. Place in the oven and cook for approximately 1 hour. You will know it is done when the pastry shrinks from the sides.

Cover and set aside for 1 hour.

Serving suggestions: Serve with a traditional Greek salad.

MARCIA'S MEATLOAF
>ROLO

INGREDIENTS

2½ lbs. Ground round
1 lb. Ground veal shoulder
1 lb. Ground pork loin
1/3 Loaf Italian bread
(inside only, no crust)
1 Large onion chopped finely
2 Stalks celery, chopped very finely
3 Eggs
Salt and pepper to taste
3 Tablespoons Parmesan cheese
or Kefalotyri cheese, grated
1 Medium tomato, chopped finely
1/3 Cup of parsley, chopped finely
6 Large white mushrooms,
chopped very finely
3 Cups ice water

Soak the bread in the ice water; squeeze dry. Using your hands, mix all of the other ingredients and the bread together in a large bowl. Shape into a loaf. Wrap the loaf in plastic wrap and refrigerate for 1 hour. Remove plastic wrap from loaf and cook at 350° for 1½ hours. Let it stand for 30 minutes. Put it back in the oven at 500° for 3 to 5 minutes to crisp the top. Serves eight.

Chef's trick: After mixing, take one tablespoon of the mixture in a small frying pan cook until well done. Let it cool and taste again to see if you need to alter the spicing.

QUICK MUSHROOM GRAVY
2 Shallots, chopped finely
8 Large white mushrooms,
chopped coarsely
1 Cup port
1½ Cups low-sodium beef broth
2 Bay leaves
1 Sprig fresh tarragon
1 Sprig fresh thyme
1 Tablespoon extra virgin olive oil
¼ Cup cold water
2 Tablespoons flour

Sauté the shallots and mushrooms in olive oil until the shallots are translucent. Add all other ingredients and cook for 30 minutes at a low simmer. Put the cold water and flour in a small glass; cover with your hand and shake well to ensure that it mixes well; add this to the mushrooms and shallots and stir over high heat to thicken.

SKEWERED MEATS
>SOUVLAKI

INGREDIENTS

For 6 people, you will need about 3 Pounds of meat.

MARINADE:
2 Tablespoons fresh flat-leaf parsley, chopped finely
2 Tablespoons fresh oregano, chopped finely
3 Cloves garlic, minced
1 Cup extra virgin olive oil
Juice of 1 lemon
Salt and pepper

Typically, Greeks prefer to do this dish with lamb; however, pork, beef, veal, or chicken is also used.

Cut the meat into 3- inch pieces. In a plastic bag, add the meat and the marinade. Refrigerate for 2 to 24 hours. Reserve the marinade.
Using metal skewers, slide the meat onto the skewers. Allow one skewer per person. Brush with the marinade.
Place on a medium heat on the grill and brush several times with the marinade.

Chef's trick: If you are using wooden skewers, be sure to soak them for at least 1 hour. Place the top of the skewer even with the top of the meat and cover the bottom of the skewer with aluminum foil to keep the skewers from burning.

Note: If you are using vegetables with your meat, marinate them as well but in a separate container to avoid cross contamination. You will want to alternate cherry tomatoes, pearl onions and chunks of peppers between each piece of meat.

Variation: Use button mushrooms and zucchini cut into chunks and alternate these with the meat.

Serving suggestions: Serve in warm pocket pita bread and top with chopped tomatoes and tzatziki sauce. Serve over couscous or rice.

PORK SHOULDER WITH ARTICHOKES
>HIRINO VRASTO ME ANGINARES

INGREDIENTS

3 Pounds of pork shoulder

3–4 Cloves garlic

Salt and pepper

½ Cup fresh flat-leaf parsley, chopped finely

1 Tablespoon fresh thyme, chopped finelywell

1 Tablespoon rosemary, chopped finely

4 Tablespoons

1 Cup dry white wine

3 Carrots, peeled and cut into 2-Inch pieces

3 Stalks celery, washed well and cut into 2-inch pieces

1 Bunch dill, chopped

2 Bunches scallions, chopped coarsely

Juice of 6 lemons

2 Eggs

1 Tablespoon cornstarch

2 Cups low-sodium, low-fat chicken broth

6 Young artichokes (or two 12 ounce cans of artichoke hearts, well drained)

Preparing the artichokes: Remove the tough outer leaves of the artichokes and trim the bottom of the stems. Cut 1 inch off the remaining leaves. Rub the artichokes with lemon juice and cut them in half lengthwise. Scrape the choke (fuzzy part) out of the hearts. Place the artichokes in cold salted water with the juice of 2 lemons; this will keep them from turning dark. Preheat the oven to 450 degrees. Wash the pork in cold water and pat dry.

Using pork shoulder: Cut the pork shoulder into 3-inch pieces. Salt and pepper the pork. Brown the pork in a skillet with olive oil. Pour off the fat before continuing. Remove the pork and put it into a large saucepan. Add the dill scallions, celery, and herbs. Cook, stirring well, until the scallions and herbs are soft. Add the white wine and cook for 5 minutes or until it has evaporated. Add the chicken broth and the pork. Cover and cook for 1 hour. Add the artichoke hearts and the carrots; continue cooking until the meat is tender.
Make Avgolemono sauce (see sauces pag 224.) and add it to the juices.

Serving suggestion: Serve over rice.

PORK CHOPS PANE
>HIRINO PANE

INGREDIENTS

6 Loin pork chops (with bone)
¼ Cup extra virgin olive oil
Salt
Freshly ground pepper
3 Large tomatoes, peeled,
seeded, and chopped coarsely
1 Cup all-purpose flour
½ Cup milk
4 Large eggs
1 Cup of Panko
(Japanese breadcrumbs)
8 Tablespoons clarified
butter or olive oil
2 Lemons, cut into wedges
1 Bunch of well-washed arugula
1 Red onion, cut into thin slices

Prepare an arugula salad by combining the tomatoes, red onion, and arugula. Do not dress the salad until just before serving.

Put each pork chop between two layers of plastic wrap and use a mallet to pound each chop to ½-inch thickness. Set aside; keep a sheet of plastic wrap between each chop. Set out three plates: one containing the flour, one containing the well-beaten eggs and milk, and one containing the Panko.

Dredge the chops in the flour; dip in the egg and milk mixture and coat with Panko. Lightly salt and pepper each chop. Keep a sheet of plastic wrap between the breaded chops.

Heat a frying pan over medium heat. Add three tablespoons of butter or olive oil and brown each side of the chops for about 4 minutes or until golden brown.

Serving suggestions: Plate the chops and dress the salad. Place the salad on top of the chops. Serve with lemon wedges.

PORK WITH CELERY AND EGG LEMON SAUCE
>HIRINO ME SELINO KE AVGOLEMONO

INGREDIENTS

3 lbs. Pork loin
2 Bunches scallions, chopped
½ Bunch fresh dill, chopped
½ Cup white wine
2 10.5 Ounce cans low-sodium
chicken broth
2 Tablespoons extra virgin olive oil
2 Tablespoons butter
1 Bunch celery, cut into
3-inch pieces
4 Eggs, separated
Juice of 2 lemons
2 Cups water
Salt and pepper to taste

Cut pork into 3-inch pieces and brown lightly in olive oil. Take pork out; add scallions and dill, and sauté for 30 seconds. Return the meat to the pot and add celery. Turn the fire to high; add the wine and cook until it evaporates. Add the chicken broth and 2 cups of water; cover and cook over low to medium fire for 1 hour. After 1 hour, turn off the flame and set aside.

In a large bowl, lightly whisk the egg whites. Add the egg yolks and incorporate. Add lemon juice and continue whisking. Uncover the pot the pork is in, and using a ladle, incorporate some of the liquid from the pork into the egg and lemon mixture, whisking constantly. Repeat the process adding another ladle of the liquid. Slowly add the egg and lemon mixture into the pot mixing with a large spoon.

Serving Suggestion: Serve with good-quality crusty bread.

Chef's trick: While incorporating the egg and lemon mixture into the pot, purse you lips and make a sucking sound. This sounds like an old wives tale but it works and keeps the eggs from curdling.

FRESH ROASTED HAM
>HIRINO PSITO

INGREDIENTS

4 Pound fresh ham
3 Cloves of garlic, cut into slivers
Salt and pepper
Juice of 1 lemon
1 Tablespoon extra virgin olive oil
**1 Stalk celery, washed and cut
into 2-inch pieces**
**1 Large carrot, washed, peeled,
and cut into 2-inch pieces**
1 Fennel bulb, sliced
**1 Medium onion,
peeled and quartered**
Water
1 Cup dry white wine

Preheat the oven to 450 degrees.

Wash the meat and pat it dry. Cut slits in the meat with a sharp paring knife, and fill each slit with a dash of salt and pepper and a sliver of garlic. Rub the surface with a lemon juice and olive oil mixture. Place the ham in a large roasting pan and put it on a pile of fennel, celery, onion, and carrot. Brown the ham in a 450-degree oven. Add a little water. Lower the oven heat to 350 degrees. Skim off the fat. Add white wine. Bake until the meat is well done and the meat thermometer registers 180 degrees. This should take about 45 minutes per pound. Add water for gravy if necessary. Be sure to de-fat the pan drippings.

ROAST SUCKLING PIG
>GOUROUNAKI STO FOURNO

INGREDIENTS

1 Suckling pig, 14 to 16 pounds
Salt and freshly ground pepper
6 Granny Smith (or other tart apple), seeded and quartered
4 Sprigs fresh thyme
2 Sprigs fresh rosemary
2 Lemons, halved
4 Stalks celery, cut into 2-inch pieces
4 Carrots, cut into 2-inch pieces
2 Medium onions, peeled and quartered
Water
Vegetable oil

Equipment: Butcher's twine, larding needle, large roasting pan with sides at least 3 inches high with a heavy-duty rack, meat thermometer, and a strong meat cleaver.

Wash the pig thoroughly and pat dry with paper towels. Season the cavity with salt and pepper; stuff it with the apples, herbs, and lemons. Close the cavity with the butcher's twine and larding needle. Tie the back feet of the pig so they are under the pig. Stretch the front feet forward. In the bottom of a large roasting pan, put the celery, carrots, and onion. Put the rack into the pan and place the pig on the rack. Brace the mouth of the pig open with a ball of aluminum foil. Cover the ears and the tail in foil to prevent burning.

Chef's trick: If the pig is not sitting straight up, you can use a brick covered in foil to help support it.

Preheat the oven to 450° F. Place the pan in the oven and pour in several cups of water. Cook the pig for 30 minutes. Reduce the heat to 350 degrees; brush the skin of the pig with vegetable oil. Roast for 30 minutes and baste again. Cover the pig with foil if it is getting too brown. Continue roasting for 2 hours. Baste with pan juices every thirty minutes. Remove the foil cover (leaving the ears covered), and cook for another 30 minutes.

Insert the meat thermometer into the thigh. The internal temperature should be 185 degrees.

Transfer the pig to a serving platter or cutting board and remove the foil.

Serving suggestions: Put an apple, fresh herbs, or flowers in the mouth for serving.

Strain and de-fat the juices. Put juices in a small saucepan and heat until they reduce. This can be used as gravy.

GRILLED PORK CHOPS
>HIRINO BRIZOLES TIS SXARAS

INGREDIENTS

6 Rib pork chops
2 Tablespoon fresh oregano or
1 teaspoon dried oregano
4 Tablespoons extra virgin olive oil
Salt and freshly ground pepper
Juice of one lemon
1 Clove garlic, finely minced
2 Tablespoons fresh parsley,
chopped finely

Have the butcher trim the rib chops so the long bone is stripped and most of the outside fat is removed. In a large zip-lock bag, put the herbs, garlic, olive oil, lemon juice, salt and pepper; add the 6 chops. Zip the bag and turn it upside down several times to fully coat the meat. Put the marinated meat in the refrigerator for 6 hours.

One half hour before cooking, remove the bag from the refrigerator to let the chops come to room temperature.

Preheat your grill to 450 degrees. Place the chops on the grill and cook 3 to 5 minutes per side. Pork should be cooked well done.

Variation: Preheat a cast iron frying pan or ridged frying pan until it smokes. Drop the chops into the pan and cook 3 to 5 minutes per side.

ALEXIS'S LOW-FAT ROAST PORK
>IGIINO HIRINO PSITO

INGREDIENTS

1 5- to 6-lb. Pork shoulder roast, boned and rolled (Ask your butcher to trim it well and tie it)
1 Clove elephant garlic, chopped finely
4 Stalks celery, broken into small pieces
1 Large Spanish onion, chopped finely
1 Tablespoon each salt and pepper
1 Tablespoon flour
1 Cup white wine
Fresh thyme (Fresh), chopped finely
Fresh parsley, chopped finely
Fresh sage, chopped finely

Mix 1 tablespoon each of salt and pepper with a clove of finely chopped garlic. With a paring knife, cut slits all over the roast; using your finger, stuff the slits with the salt, pepper, and garlic mixture. Rub the outside of the roast with a mixture of thyme, sage, and freshly chopped parsley.

Using a high flame, brown the outside of the roast on all sides in the stockpot.

Place the lid on the pot and allow the roast to cook over a low flame for one hour, checking frequently. The juices of the roast should give enough liquid, but if not, add a little wine.

After one hour, add the celery and the chopped onion, and continue to simmer for 45 minutes.

Remove the roast. Add the wine and let cook over a high heat for 2 to 3 minutes, or until the alcohol burns off.

Chef's trick: Add ½ cup of cold water mixed with 1 tablespoon of flour. (To remove lumps, put your hand over the top of the cup of water and flour mixture and shake vigorously for one minute.) Add to the juices and stir until the sauce is thickened.

Serving suggestion: Serve with rice pilaf.
(Serves 6 to 8.)

BEEF STEW WITH POTATOES AND ZUCCHINI
>BODINO KATSAROLAS ME PATATES KE KOLOKITHIA

INGREDIENTS

3 Pounds chuck beef, cut into 3-Inch cubes
2 Large red onions, diced
2 Stalks celery, cut into 1-inch pieces
2 Sprigs thyme
2 Bay leaves
2 Tablespoons all-purpose flour
6 Large Yukon Gold potatoes, peeled and quartered
4 Large zucchini, cut into ¼-inch rounds
2 Medium tomatoes, peeled and seeded
3 Tablespoons vegetable oil
1 10.5 Ounce can beef broth
6 Cups water
1 Tablespoon olive oil
Salt and freshly ground black pepper to taste

In a large Dutch oven, sear the meat on all sides in vegetable oil. Remove the meat and set aside. Add the onion, tomatoes, celery, bay leaves, and thyme.

Cook until the onions are translucent. Pour off any excess fat. Put the meat back in the pot and add the wine. Over a high fire, let the alcohol evaporate for 2 minutes. Add the flour and stir well. Add the beef broth and 6 cups of water. Cover well and cook for 1¾ hours, or until the beef is tender.

In a baking dish, place the potatoes and zucchini in a little oil and bake in a 400-degree oven until lightly browned. Add them to the stew and cook for 30 minutes or until the potatoes are done. Turn off the heat and let stand for 30 minutes.

Serving suggestions: Serve over rice or serve with fresh country bread and a plate of Feta cheese drizzled with extra virgin olive oil and dusted with thyme.

Chef's trick: If you don't want to take the time to skin and seed the tomatoes, you can use Roma tomatoes chopped finely.

BOILED BEEF DINNER
>VRASTO KREAS

INGREDIENTS

**3 Pounds chuck beef,
cut into 3-Inch cubes
2 Large red onions, diced
2 Stalks celery,
cut into1-inch pieces
2 Sprigs thyme
2 Bay leaves
2 Tablespoons all-purpose flour
6 Large Yukon Gold potatoes,
peeled and quartered
4 Large carrots, peeled and cut
into 2-inch pieces
2 Medium tomatoes,
peeled and seeded
3 Tablespoons vegetable oil
1 10.5 Ounce can beef broth
6 Cups water
Salt and freshly ground
pepper to taste**

In a large Dutch oven, sear the meat on all sides in vegetable oil. Remove the meat and set aside. Add the onion, tomatoes, celery, bay leaves, and thyme.
Cook until the onions are translucent. Pour off any excess fat. Put the meat back in the pot and add the wine. Over a high fire, let the alcohol evaporate for 2 minutes. Add the flour and stir well. Add the beef broth and 6 cups of water. Cover well and cook for 1¾ hours, or until the beef is tender.
In a separate frying pan, cook the potatoes and carrots in a little oil until browned.
Add them to the stew and cook for 30 minutes, or until the potatoes are done. Turn off the heat and let stand for 30 minutes.

Serving suggestions: Serve over rice, or serve with fresh country bread and a plate of Feta cheese drizzled with extra virgin olive oil and dusted with thyme.

Chef's trick: If you don't want to take the time to skin and seed the tomatoes, you can use Roma tomatoes and chop them before putting them into the sauce.

LEFKAS POT ROAST
>TIS KATSAROLAS

INGREDIENTS

3–4 Pounds of meat
(ask the butcher to tie it well)
½ Cup celery
½ Cup carrots, chopped finely
½ Cup sweet onion, chopped finely
2 Whole garlic cloves, cut into slices
Olive oil
2 Tablespoons fresh parsley,
chopped finely
½ Teaspoon lemon zest
1 10.5 Ounce can beef
or chicken broth
1 Cup white wine
2 Tablespoons flour
Water
2 Cloves garlic, chopped finely
Bouquet de Garni (a sprig each
of thyme, parsley, and rosemary,
tied together at the stems with
butcher's twine)
Salt and pepper

This recipe is good for all types of pot roast (beef, veal, or pork)

Make small slits in the roast and stuff each slit with a mixture of salt, pepper, and slices of garlic. Using a large pot that can be covered tightly, brown the roast in two tablespoons of olive oil. Be sure to brown it on all sides in a hot pan. Remove the roast and set aside. Add the celery, onion, garlic, and carrots; sauté over a low fire until they are translucent. Into the pot, add the broth, 1 cup water, and 1 cup white wine, the lemon zest and the meat. Cover well and put into a 350-degree oven for 1½ hour. Check often to be sure there is enough liquid. Add water if needed.

Remove the meat. Strain the liquid and de-fat it. Put it back into the pot. Briskly whisk 2 tablespoons of flour into ½ cup water; whisk until there are no lumps. On top of the stove, add flour mixture to the pot; mix well and allow it to thicken.

Slice the meat against the grain. Pour the sauce over the meat. Sprinkle with the finely chopped parsley.

Note: If you are using beef, you should ask the butcher for chuck; if using veal, ask for leg of veal; and if using pork, ask for the leg of fresh pork.

BEEF STEW WITH POTATOES AND CARROTS
>BODINO KATSAROLAS ME PATATES KE KAROTA

INGREDIENTS

1 4-Pound chuck roast or brisket
4 Carrots, peeled and cut into 2-Inch pieces
2 Stalks celery, washed and cut into 2-inch pieces
1 Cup low-sodium, low-fat chicken broth
4 Cups beef broth or water
5 Whole peppercorns
1 Large onion, halved
3 Fresh bay leaves
1 Sprig fresh thyme
½ Cup dry white wine
2 Tablespoons extra virgin olive oil
24 Small Yukon Gold potatoes, peeled
1 Large tomato, cut into quarters
Salt and pepper to taste
4 Cups water

In a large saucepan, caramelize the meat in 2 tablespoons olive oil. Add all of the other ingredients except the potatoes.

Cover tightly and braise in a 350-degree oven for 1½ to 2 hours, or until the meat is tender. You can also cook this dish on top of the stove over a medium flame. Remove the meat and set aside. Strain the sauce and add the meat and potatoes. Cook covered tightly on top of the stove for about 20 minutes or until the potatoes are soft.

Variations: You can also prepare veal shoulder, veal chops, lamb shoulder, leg of lamb, or rack of lamb using the same method.

Serving Suggestions:
1. Serve with Feta cheese and fresh crusty bread.
2. Serve with a sauce made with the juice of ½ lemon, 1 teaspoon grainy mustard, 4 tablespoons of extra virgin olive oil, and chopped fresh parsley. Mix well.

VEAL STEW WITH PEARL ONIONS
>STIFADO

INGREDIENTS

**4 Pounds stew veal,
cut into 2-Inch pieces
3 Pounds pearl onions, peeled
½ Cup red wine
3 Tablespoons red wine vinegar
4 Cups water
1 10.5 Ounce can low-sodium,
low-fat chicken broth
4 Tablespoons all-purpose flour
4 Bay leaves
1 Sprig rosemary, remove the
leaves and chop finely
3 Tablespoons extra virgin olive oil
3 Tablespoons butter
Salt and fresh-ground black
pepper to taste**

Dredge the meat lightly in flour, and shake off the excess flour. Brown the meat in a skillet with olive oil. When the meat is caramelized nicely, add the wine and the vinegar until they evaporate. Add the chicken broth, water, bay leaves, and rosemary. Cook over a low fire, covered, for 1 hour and 30 minutes or until the meat is very tender. In a separate skillet, cook the onions in butter over a very low fire until they are golden brown and caramelized well. Add the onions to the meat mixture for the last 20 minutes of cooking.

Serving suggestions: Serve over pasta or rice. Serve with good-quality crusty bread.

Chef's trick: With a sharp paring knife, make a cross on the bottom of the onions. Be careful not to cut into the meat. Drop them in boiling water for 1 minute. This will make them easier to peel.

VEAL STEW WITH STRING BEANS
>MOSCARI ME FRESCA FASOULIA

INGREDIENTS

3 Pounds of cubed veal from the leg
3 Tablespoons extra virgin olive oil
1 Tablespoon all-purpose flour
6 Medium tomatoes,
chopped finely grated
1 Large onion, chopped finely
1 Clove garlic, chopped finely
1 Cup dry, white wine
2 Tablespoons fresh parsley,
chopped finely
3 Cups water
2 Pounds fresh or frozen
string beans, with the tips cut off

Brown the meat in 2 tablespoons of olive oil. Reserve the meat and pour off all but 1 tablespoon of the oil. Add the other tablespoon of olive oil and sauté the onions until translucent. Add the garlic and cook for 30 seconds. Add one tablespoon of flour and mix. Return the meat to the pot; add the wine, tomato, and 1 tablespoon parsley. Add the water. Cook over a medium fire for 1 hour, add the string beans and continue cooking for 20 minutes.

GRILLED VEAL CHOPS
>PSITES BRIZOLES MOSHARISIES

INGREDIENTS

6 Rib veal chops
2 Tablespoon fresh oregano,
chopped finely
1 Teaspoon dried oregano
4 Tablespoons extra virgin olive oil
Salt and fresh-ground pepper
Juice of one lemon
1 Clove garlic, finely minced
2 Tablespoons fresh parsley,
chopped finely

Have the butcher trim the rib chops so the long bone is stripped and most of the outside fat removed. In a large zip-lock bag, combine the herbs, garlic, olive oil, lemon juice, salt, and pepper; add the chops. Zip the bag and turn it upside down several times to fully coat the meat. Put the marinated meat in the refrigerator for 6 hours.

A half hour before cooking, remove the bag from the refrigerator. Let the chops come to room temperature. Preheat your grill to 450 degrees. Place the chops on the grill and cook 2 to 3 minutes per side for medium-well-done chops.

Variation: Preheat a cast iron frying pan or ridged frying pan until it smokes. Drop the chops into the pan and cook 2 to 3 minutes per side.

FILET MIGNON OF VEAL TENDERLOIN
>BON FILET MOSHARIOU

INGREDIENTS

1 3-lb. Veal tenderloin, cut into 12 2-inch rounds. (You may have to ask your butcher to order this for you)
Salt and pepper to taste
1 Tablespoon extra virgin olive oil

In a large frying pan, get the oil hot enough to smoke. Add the tenderloins and brown 3 minutes on each side for medium rare. Remove from the pan and set aside.

SAUCE
1 Cup celery, chopped finely
1 Cup carrots, chopped finely
1 Cup onion, chopped finely
1 Cup leeks, chopped finely
1 Tablespoon shallot, chopped finely
1 Tablespoon sage, chopped finely
1 Sprig thyme, chopped finely
¼ Cup flat-leaf parsley, chopped finely
2 Cups red wine
2 Cups veal stock (preferably homemade)
1 Cup chicken stock
4 oz. Julienne Virginia ham
2 Strips bacon, diced

In a medium saucepan, brown the bacon. Remove the bacon. Sauté the first eight ingredients in the bacon fat until the onions are translucent. Add the wine and put over high heat for 2 minutes. Add the stock. Cook for 1 hour over a medium fire with the lid off. Let the sauce reduce by 75 percent. Strain the sauce to remove the vegetables.

Serving Suggestion: This dish is best served with the pasta with peas and mushrooms recipe on page 202.

VEAL CHOPS WITH ANCHOVIES
>PANE MOSCHARI ME ANCHOVIES

INGREDIENTS

9 Fresh eggs
6 Veal chops, rib
12 Anchovies
1 Cup all-purpose flour
1 Cup fresh toasted bread crumbs
(unseasoned)
¼ Cup Kefalotyri, grated
2 Tablespoons extra virgin olive oil

Using a sharp knife, cut away the meat from the top of the bone to expose it. Stop where the wide part of the meat starts. Trim away any outside membrane and fat. Place a sheet of plastic wrap on a flat counter or cutting board; place one chop on the plastic wrap and cover it with another sheet of plastic wrap. Pound each chop flat with a mallet. It should end up almost double in size. Put the chops on a large plate and set aside. Mix the breadcrumbs and the cheese on a large plate. In a flat pan, beat three eggs well. Take each chop and dip it in flour. Shake off excess flour. Dip each chop in the egg, then in the breadcrumbs. Be sure each chop is well coated. Stack the chops on a plate with a sheet of plastic wrap between the layers. Wash 12 anchovies in cold water to remove some of the saltiness.

In a large frying pan, heat the oil to medium hot. Place the flattened chops in the oil and fry until golden brown. Remove and drain on paper towels. When all of the chops are done, fry the 6 eggs individually. Put the cooked chops on individual plates for serving and top with a fried egg and 2 anchovies. Serve with lemon wedges.

Variations: Instead of the eggs and anchovies, this dish can be served topped with pieces of basil and chopped tomatoes or with fresh arugula.

Chef's trick: Do not chop basil; it will bruise. It is best to tear the leaves instead.

VEAL SHANKS
>MOSCARI KOKINISTO

INGREDIENTS

4 Veal shanks, about 2 inches
thick (ask the butcher to tie them)
4 to 6 Celery stalks,
cut into large pieces
3 to 4 Carrots, cut into large pieces
1 Large onion, quartered
3 Cloves
½ Stick cinnamon
1 Large leek, chopped finely
3 to 4 Tomatoes, chopped course
1 10.5 Ounce can chicken broth
1 10.5 Ounce can beef broth
1 Cup water
12 Garlic cloves (whole, peeled,
and slightly smashed)
1 Tablespoon olive oil
2 Tablespoons all-purpose flour
½ Cup chopped parsley
1 Stalk fresh rosemary
White wine (1 cup)

Dust the shanks with flour and salt and pepper. Brown the shanks in a large saucepan in 3-4 tablespoons olive oil. Remove the meat and set aside. Increase the heat and add the vegetables. Cook the vegetables while shaking the pot for about 5 minutes. Add a tablespoon of butter and shake again. Add the garlic and stir. Add the beef and the liquids. Add pepper, cloves, cinnamon, and rosemary, and cover. Put in the 350° oven for 2 to 2½ hours (or until meat falls off the bone).

POULTRY

KOTOPOULO

CHICKEN STUFFED WITH SPINACH AND FETA CHEESE
>GEMISTO KOTOPOULO ME SPANAKI KE FETA

INGREDIENTS

1 5-Pound free-range roasting chicken
¼ Pound feta cheese
1 Pound fresh baby spinach
2 Scallions
1 Tablespoon fresh parsley, chopped finely
1 Teaspoon fresh dill, chopped finely
2 Tablespoons extra virgin olive oil
1 Tablespoon Fytini or margarine
1 Cup dry white wine
1 Stalk celery, chopped in 1-inch pieces
2 Cloves garlic, minced
1 10.5 Ounce can low-sodium, low-fat chicken broth
Salt and pepper to taste

Preheat the oven to 350 degrees.

Wash the chicken well inside and out. Pat it dry with paper towels. In a small skillet, sauté the spinach, parsley, scallions, and dill until the spinach is wilted and the scallions are translucent. Set it aside to cool for 20 minutes. Mix the cheese and the spinach mixture together. Using your hand, very gingerly loosen the breast and thigh skin from the meat of the chicken, being careful not to split the skin. Insert the mixture under the skin. Tie the legs of the chicken together and rub the outside of the chicken with the margarine and the rest of the olive oil. Rub the outside of the chicken with salt and pepper.

In the bottom of a roasting pan, place the garlic, celery, and chicken broth. Put the chicken on top of the celery and garlic, and roast for 40 minutes. Add the white wine and continue cooking for 20 minutes. Turn up the heat to 450 degrees and roast for an additional 15 minutes or until the skin is nice and crispy.

Serving suggestion: Serve with roasted potatoes and a nice green salad.

Chef's trick: Do not overfill the cavity. There should only be about ¼ inch of the mixture spread evenly under the skin. When you have finished filling the cavity you made, use a spatula to press down lightly on the skin.

CHICKEN WITH ONIONS AND PEPPERS
>KOUTOPOULO ME KREMIDIA KE PIPERIES

INGREDIENTS

**1 4–5 Pound chicken, washed
well, inside and out
3 Red peppers,
seeded and cut into strips
3 Yellow peppers,
seeded and cut into strips
2 Large sweet onions, peeled and
cut into ¼-inch rings
4 Cloves garlic, minced
2 Tablespoons all-purpose flour
3 Tablespoons olive oil
½ Cup dry white wine
2 10.5 Ounce cans low-sodium,
low-fat chicken broth
4 Large tomatoes, peeled,
seeded and diced
2 Bay leaves
2 Tablespoons fresh thyme,
chopped finely
1 Shallot, minced
2 Tablespoons butter
Salt and pepper to taste**

Remove the package of giblets from the cavity. Cut the chicken into 8 pieces. Dredge the chicken in flour and salt and pepper. Brown the chicken well in olive oil in a "Dutch" oven. Remove the chicken and set aside. Add 2 tablespoons of butter to the remaining oil and sauté the peppers, onion, shallots, bay leaves, and thyme in a large saucepan. Add the garlic and cook for 1 minute. Turn up the heat and add the white wine. Cook for 1 minute. Add the tomatoes, chicken broth and 1 cup water. Add the chicken and bring to a boil. Lower the heat and cover the pot. Let the chicken and sauce simmer for 1 hour and 15 minutes.

Serving suggestions: Serve this stew over spaghetti with a good-quality grated Parmesan or Kefalotyri cheese.

ROAST CHICKEN WITH GREEK SPICES AND ROASTED POTATOES
>PSITO ELLINIKO KOTOPOULO ME PATATES

INGREDIENTS

1 4-lb Chicken, washed thoroughly
1 Stick soft butter
4 Sprigs fresh thyme
2 Lemons
Salt and pepper
4 Stalks celery, cut into 2-inch pieces
1 Head garlic
½ Cup white wine
2 Cups chicken broth
6 Large Yukon Gold potatoes

Squeeze the juice of one lemon on the outside of the chicken. Cut the second lemon into two pieces and put into the cavity. Rub the outside of the chicken with the softened butter all over. Salt and pepper to taste. Put 2 sprigs of thyme in the cavity. Strip the remaining sprigs of thyme over the outside of the chicken. Tie the legs and wings of the chicken. Place the chicken in the refrigerator for one hour or until the butter is firm.

Note: You can easily roast potatoes with the chicken. Peel and cut the potatoes into 6 pieces (cut them lengthwise).
Place the peeled and cut potatoes in a bowl of cold water in the refrigerator for 1 hour. Pour off the water. This reduces the starch and allows the potatoes to become crispier. Salt and pepper to taste. Place potatoes around the chicken before you put the chicken in the oven.

Chef's trick: Put the celery in the bottom of a roasting pan. Cut the head of garlic in half so that the garlic cloves are exposed. Put half of the head of garlic in the middle of the pan and rest the chicken on top of the garlic. Add the white wine and chicken broth.
Preheat the oven to 400°. Cook the chicken at 400° for 15 minutes. Reduce the heat to 350° and cook until the thermometer reaches 160° when inserted. This should be about 1½ hours.

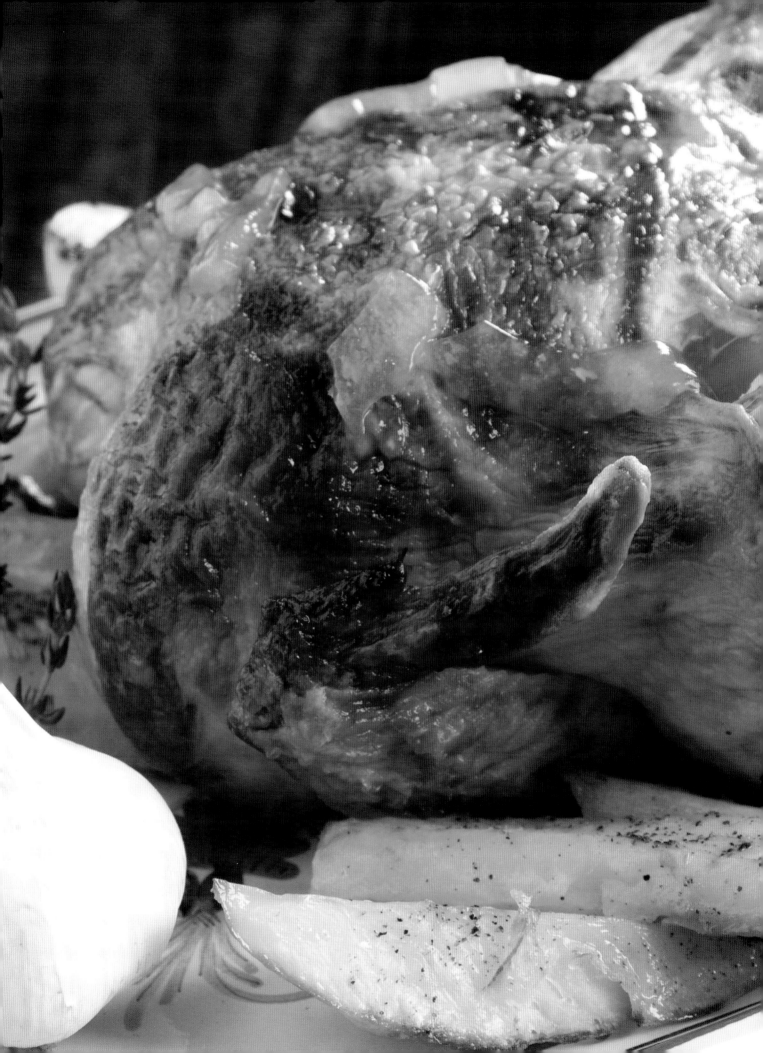

CHICKEN STEW
>KOTOPOULO YACHNI

INGREDIENTS

1 4- to 5-lb. Chicken,
cut into eight pieces
1 Tablespoon extra virgin olive oil
1 Large onion, diced finely
2 Tablespoons flour
1 Tablespoon butter
1½ Cups white wine
3 Large ripe tomatoes, diced finely
1 Tablespoon tomato paste
2 Cups low-sodium chicken broth
2 Cups water
3 Bay leaves
1 Sprig fresh thyme
5 Allspice berries

Using the olive oil, brown the chicken pieces in a Dutch oven. Remove the chicken and reserve. Add the onions to the same pot and sauté until translucent. Add the butter and flour; stir until the roux turns a caramel color. Add the chicken. Add the white wine and let it cook over a low fire until the wine evaporates. Turn off the heat. Incorporate the remaining ingredients. Cover and let simmer for 1 to 1¼ hours. Let it cool and remove the surface fat. Re-heat and serve over pasta.

Chef's trick: If the sauce appears too thin, use two tablespoons of flour and ¼ cup of cold water. Stir well and add to the sauce to thicken it. Be sure the mixture has time for the flour to cook before serving.

Serving suggestion: This dish is best if served with a light sprinkle of Parmesan cheese and some good crusty bread.

PROHIBITION CHICKEN
OR BROWN BAG CHICKEN
>KLEFTIKO KOTOPOULO

INGREDIENTS

**1 2½-lb. Free-range chicken
3 Large baking potatoes,
peeled, cut into eights
½ Cup celery, chopped1 teaspoon
fresh thyme, chopped finely
1 Teaspoon fresh rosemary,
chopped finely
1 Teaspoon fresh-ground
black pepper
1 Teaspoon fresh parsley,
chopped finely
1 Teaspoon fresh oregano,
chopped finely
1 Lemon
1 Large clove garlic
1 Tablespoon Fytani or margarine
½ Cup white wine**

Wash the chicken thoroughly, removing giblets and any observed fat. Pat dry. Put 2 stalks celery and ½ lemon in the cavity. Squeeze ½ lemon on top. Coat the chicken in a mixture of the herbs and pepper. Dot the chicken with margarine, and place in a brown grocery bag. Put diced celery, potatoes, and garlic in the bag with the chicken. Fold the bag tightly and tie closed with cooking twine.

Preheat oven to 400°. Place the brown bag with the vegetables and chicken in a roasting pan in the oven for 1/2 hour. Reduce the heat to 350°; continue cooking for 1½ hours. The bag may smell as if it is burning; however, the juices from the chicken will keep it safe. Do not open the bag to check on the chicken until the last few minutes. Carefully remove the bag; it will have steam inside. Leave the chicken and vegetables in the roaster. Add ½ cup white wine. Put it back in the oven. Turn the oven to 500° for ten minutes to crisp the outside of the chicken.

NOTE: Do not be afraid that the bag will catch on fire. The juice of the chicken will keep it moist. Be sure the bag does not have any printing on it because the ink may not be safe to ingest.

WILD GAME

ROAST DUCK
>PSITI PAPIA

INGREDIENTS

2 Large ducks
2 Apples, quartered
2 Medium onions, quartered
4 Sprigs rosemary
Salt and freshly ground pepper
Extra virgin olive oil
½ Stick butter

Wash the ducks well inside and out. Remove the giblets.

Chef's trick:
Poaching the ducks helps to eliminate the fat under the skin and it keeps the meat juicy. The broth can be used as stock. For a really rich stock, start with a 10.5 ounce can of low-fat, low-sodium chicken broth and water, and bring it to a boil in a large stockpot. The stock can be frozen for future use.

Prick the duck's skin thoroughly with the tines of a fork. Be sure there is enough stock to completely cover the ducks. Add the ducks to the pot (open end down) so it fills with stock and stays on the bottom. Bring the stock back to a boil. Place something heavy on the ducks so they stay submerged. Lower the heat and gently simmer uncovered for 30 to 45 minutes.

Remove the ducks and set aside. Preheat the oven to 375 degrees. Take 2 to 3 tablespoons of duck fat off the top of the stock. Strain the stock and reserve it. Grease the bottom of a large roasting pan with the duck fat. Place the apple, onion, and 1 sprig of the rosemary in the cavity of each duck with salt and pepper. Be careful not to break the skin on the ducks; it is delicate. Tie the ducks by taking cooking twine and going twice around the wings; then, bring it over the legs and tie the legs tightly so the cavity stays closed. Brush the ducks with a mixture of extra virgin olive oil and clarified butter.

Place the ducks breast side up in the roasting pan. Salt and pepper them. Move them around in the fat so they don't stick.
Roast for 45 minutes. Note: If there is too much fat accumulating in the bottom of the pan, using a spoon remove some of the fat.

Serving suggestions: Serve with Wild Game Bird sauce (See sauces.)

DUCK SALMI
>PAPIA SALMI

INGREDIENTS

**3 Wild ducks
(Muscovy or Mallard)
Juice of 2 lemons
6 Sprigs fresh thyme
2 Sprigs fresh rosemary
2 Tablespoons fresh parsley,
chopped finely
¼ Cup red wine vinegar
4 Tablespoons extra virgin olive oil
1 Tablespoon butter
1 Whole onion, grated
6 Cloves garlic, minced
½ Cup dry white wine**

This recipe is from my sister, Panagiota. It has never been recorded before and has been handed down in my family for generations.

Wash the ducks inside and out. Remove the giblets. Reserve the liver. Cut each duck into eight pieces. Place the duck in a large ceramic bowl filled with equal parts cold water and club soda. Add the juice of one whole lemon. Refrigerate for 3 hours.
Put 2 tablespoons of olive oil in a Dutch oven and brown the duck pieces over a medium heat. Remove the duck and discard the oil. Put the duck back in the Dutch oven and add 1 tablespoon olive oil, onion, and garlic, wine, and vinegar, and 1 tablespoon each of parsley, rosemary, and thyme. Cover the pot tightly and cook over a low fire. Turn the duck pieces every ten minutes for a half hour. Add a tablespoon of butter and a tablespoon olive oil and continue cooking for another 30 minutes.
Take the duck out and set it aside. Strain and de-fat the remaining liquid. Put the duck back with the liquid and turn the fire up to high for 1 minute. Squeeze the juice of a lemon over the duck.

Serving suggestions: Sprinkle a tablespoon of fresh finely chopped parsley over the duck. Serve with wild rice or French fries and salad.

BONELESS PRESSED QUAIL
>PSITA ORTYKIA

INGREDIENTS

12 Quail (two per person)
12 Slices of pancetta
12 Sprigs of fresh thyme
Juice of 2 lemons
2 Tablespoons extra virgin olive oil
Salt and pepper to taste

Preparing the quail: Remove the wings and set aside. Leave the legs intact. Using a small boning knife, cut the back open to lay the birds flat. Cut away the backbone. Slide the knife blade under the ribs on both sides of each bird and use your hands to remove the ribs and the breastbone. Leave as much meat as possible.
In a large frying pan, render the pancetta and set it aside. Place the flattened quail in the frying pan, skin-side up, and press down on them with a wide spatula. Cook over a hot fire for three minutes on each side. Squeeze the lemon juice over the quail just before serving.

Serving suggestions: The quail can be served over polenta, wild rice, or orzo mixed with a tablespoon of extra virgin olive oil and a tablespoon of chopped fresh chives. Serves six

GRAINS
& PASTA

CALAMARI WITH MACARONI
>KALAMARAKI ME MACARONI

INGREDIENTS

**3 Pounds calamari
(both the tentacles and body).
3 Tablespoons extra virgin olive oil
2 Bunches scallions,
chopped finely
3 Tablespoons fresh flat-leaf
parsley, chopped finely
3 Stalks celery, chopped finely
3 Large cloves garlic, minced finely
½ Cup dry white wine
Juice of ¼ lemon
2 Cups water
Salt and pepper
1 Pound penne or small macaroni**

Sauté the squid in olive oil for two minutes until it turns red. Add everything else except the wine. Cook over a medium fire for 3 minutes, stirring constantly. Add the wine; cook for one minute or until it evaporates. Add two cups of water. Cover tightly and cook over a low-to-medium fire for 1 hour. Add the macaroni. Cover the pot and cook for 8 minutes or until all the liquid is absorbed. Squeeze the juice of ¼ of a lemon over the top.

Serving Suggestion: Serve with good-quality crusty bread.

FRESH CORN POLENTA
>FRESCO CALABOKI POLENTA

INGREDIENTS

**16 Ears fresh corn
½ Stick butter
½ Cup milk
Salt and fresh-ground pepper**

With a sharp chef's knife, remove the kernels from the cobs. Put the corn in a food processor. Use the sharp blade and pulse three or four times, or until the corn is a mush. Add the butter and the milk and pulse again. Using a large saucepan, cook the mush over a medium heat, stirring continuously until the mush is a thick, creamy texture.
This dish has a natural sweetness due to the high fructose content of corn.
Add salt and pepper to taste.

RICE PILAF
>RYZI PILAFI

INGREDIENTS

2 Small shallots, peeled and chopped finely
1 Tablespoon butter
1 Tablespoon extra virgin olive oil
1 Bay leaf
1 Can of low-fat, low-sodium chicken broth
1 Cup long-grain rice (Uncle Ben's)
Water

In a medium saucepan, sauté the shallots and bay leaf in butter and olive oil for 1 minute. Add the rice and toast, stirring constantly, for two minutes. Add the chicken broth and water as needed. Bring to a rolling boil and cook, uncovered, until most of the liquid is reduced to the same height in the pot as the rice. Cover tightly and remove from the stove. In a preheated oven, cook the rice for 20 minutes at 400° degrees.

Chef's trick: In order to determine the amount of liquid required to cook the rice, add the chicken broth, and then a can of water. You may need to add more water. The liquid needs to be two fingers above the rice when you start it boiling.

Variations: Add ¼ cup of toasted pine nuts to the rice when it has finished cooking.

PASTA WITH PEAS AND MUSHROOMS
>MAKARONIA ME BIZELIA KE MANITARIA

INGREDIENTS

¼ Cup English peas
1 Shallot, chopped finely
1 Clove garlic, chopped finely
4 Ounces Chanterelle or Porcini
mushrooms, chopped finely
¼ Teaspoon truffle butter
½ Cup white wine
1 Tablespoon butter
1 Tablespoon extra virgin olive oil
1 Pound fettuccini

In a medium frying pan, sauté the mushrooms in butter. Add the shallots and garlic. Sauté until the shallots are translucent. Add the white wine and truffle butter. Allow to simmer.

In a large stockpot, bring water to a rolling boil. Add 1 teaspoon salt. Add the fettuccine. Allow the pasta to boil for about 10 minutes or until al dente.

Add the peas to the pasta sauce and cook for two minutes. Drain the pasta in a colander. Add the pasta to the sauce and toss.

CREAMY CORN MEAL
>POLENTA

INGREDIENTS

1 Cup milk
2 Cups chicken broth
¾ Cup corn meal
1 Tablespoon fresh chive,
chopped finely
1 Tablespoon butter
or extra virgin olive oil

In a medium saucepan, scald the milk and chicken broth. Do not let it boil. Using a wire whisk, stir in the corn meal. Stir constantly until it becomes thick and creamy. (The desired consistency is similar to loose mashed potatoes.) Mix in the salt and pepper and chives.

Variations: This dish can be served either soft or firm. Soft polenta can be served under wild game birds, veal shanks, chicken, or stews.

To firm the polenta, pour the hot polenta into a flat pan about 2½ inches deep. The firm polenta is accomplished by refrigerating the cooked polenta for one hour. Cut the firm polenta into 3-inch squares and sauté in a little butter or olive oil until lightly brown on both sides.

The warm polenta can be poured into a lightly greased mold such as a cupcake mold and baked at 350 degrees for 15 to 20 minutes or until golden brown.

OCTOPUS STEW WITH PASTA
>PULPO KE ZITI

INGREDIENTS

**3 Pounds baby octopus, both
tentacles and body
3 Tablespoons Extra Virgin Olive Oil
2 Bunches scallions,
chopped finely
3 Tablespoons fresh parsley,
chopped finely
3 Stalks celery, chopped finely
3 Large cloves garlic,
chopped finely
½ Cup white wine
2 Cups water
2 Medium tomatoes,
chopped fine
1 Teaspoon tomato paste
12 Kalamata olives,
pitted and rinsed well
½ Teaspoon red pepper flakes
Salt and Pepper to taste
1 Pound of Ziti**

Sauté the octopus in olive oil for two minutes or until it turns red. Add everything else except the wine. Cook over a medium fire for 3 minutes, stirring constantly. Add the wine and cook for one minute or until the wine evaporates. Add tomatoes, tomato paste, red pepper flakes and two cups of water. Cover tightly and cook over a low to medium fire for 1 hour. Add the olives and cook for five more minutes.

Bring 4 quarts of water to a boil. Add ½ teaspoon sea salt. Add the Ziti and cook 8 – 10 minutes or until the pasta is al dente.

Serving Suggestions: Serve the octopus over Ziti with good quality crusty bread.

GREEK PASTA AND CHEESE
>ELINIKI MAKARONADA ME TYRI

INGREDIENTS

1½ Packages small macaroni
or penne
½ Teaspoon nutmeg
2 Shallots, chopped finely
3 Tablespoons extra virgin olive oil
4 Cup milk
2 Bay leaves
8 Tablespoons butter
1 Cup all-purpose flour
2 Large eggs, beaten well
½ Cup milk
1 Cup of grated cheese,
use a mix of any of these cheeses:
Kefalotyri
Parmesan
Kasseri
Ricotta (dry)

Sauté shallots in olive oil until translucent. Boil the pasta until al dente; strain and rinse in hot water. Oil the bottom of an ovenproof pan and add a layer of pasta and the shallots; then add half of the cheese and nutmeg. Add a layer of pasta and top with more of the cheese. Make a béchamel sauce (see sauces) and pour over the top. Top with the rest of the cheese. Bake it in the oven at 375 degrees for 30 minutes.

MUSHROOM RAVIOLI
WITH TRUFFLE BUTTER AND SAGE
>MANITARIA RAVIOLI ME TRUFFLE VOUTIRO KE FASCOMILO

INGREDIENTS

3 to 4 Tablespoons high quality salted butter
24 Fresh sage leaves
½ Cup milk
1 Tablespoon all-purpose flour
1 Teaspoon truffle butter
½ Cup grated good-quality Parmesan or Kefalotyri cheese
36 Fresh mushroom ravioli

Bring a large pot of water to a boil. Add 1 teaspoon of salt. Add the ravioli. When the ravioli rises to the top, it is done. Remove and keep warm by covering with aluminum foil. In a large frying pan, melt the butter and the truffle butter. Add the sage leaves and fry until crispy. Set the sage aside and also to dry on paper towels. Add the flour and stir well. Add the milk and continue stirring with a wire whisk until you have a creamy sauce. Add the ravioli and heat until the ravioli is hot. Serve on large plates and use the sage leaves to decorate the plates. Sprinkle with Parmesan cheese and grind fresh pepper over the top.

BAKED PASTA WITH MEAT SAUCE
>PASTITSIO

Baked Pasta with meat sauce is time-consuming to make. It can; however, be made the day before and re-heated in the oven. It is made in three steps. Make the meat sauce first. Then make the béchamel sauce while the pasta is boiling.

MEAT SAUCE/ KYMAS
(see sauces pag 219)

Step 1: Make the meat sauce

BÉCHAMEL SAUCE
(see sauces pag 223

Step 2: Make the Béchamel Sauce on pag

INGREDIENTS

1 Pound of ziti
2 Eggs lightly beaten
3 Tablespoons of grated
Parmesan or Kefalotyri cheese
1 Cup of béchamel sauce

2 Tablespoons melted butter
1/2-Cup plain breadcrumbs
¼ Teaspoon grated nutmeg
¼ Cup grated Parmesan or Kefalotyri cheese

Step 3: PASTA/ MAKARONIA: In a large saucepan, bring the salted water to a boil. Add the pasta and simmer for 10 minutes or until al dente. Drain in a colander and transfer to a large bowl. Allow to cool and then add the beaten eggs, cheese and béchamel sauce. Toss the pasta until well coated.

TO ASSEMBLE THE PASTITSIO: Preheat the oven to 350. Brush the bottom and sides to a rectangular 11x14 baking dish with the melted butter. Sprinkle with breadcrumbs. Spread 1/3 of the pasta evenly in the dish. Add ½ cup béchamel sauce. Drain the meat sauce and reserve the liquid. Cover the pasta with the meat sauce. Spread the remaining pasta over the top and spoon on the béchamel sauce, smoothing it over the top. Sprinkle lightly with nutmeg and grated cheese. Bake for 40-45 minutes or until the top is golden brown. Leave to rest for 20 minutes before cutting into individual squares. Re-heat the reserved liquid from the meat sauce and spoon a little over each portion

PENNE PASTA WITH ARUGULA AND PROSCIUTTO
>KOFTO MAKARONI ME ROCA KE PROSCIUTTO

INGREDIENTS

1 Pound penne pasta
3 Ounces Prosciutto de Parma, chopped coarsely
1 Shallot, peeled and minced
½ Cup chicken broth
2 Tablespoons extra virgin olive oil
1 Tablespoon butter
1 Tablespoon fresh flat-leaf parsley chopped finely
1 Tablespoon fresh chives, chopped finely
½ Cup Parmesan cheese, grated
½ Cup dry white wine
1 Bunch arugula, washed and dried well, and chopped coarsely
1 Medium tomato, peeled, seeded, and chopped finely

Put 4 quarts of water on to boil. Add 1 teaspoon of salt. When the water comes to a rolling boil, add the pasta and cook until almost soft.

At the same time, in a medium frying pan, sauté the shallot in 1 tablespoon butter and 1 tablespoon olive oil until translucent. Add the prosciutto and cook for 1 minute. Add the tomato and white wine. Allow the alcohol to evaporate (about 3 minutes). Add the chives, parsley and ½ cup of chicken broth. Bring to a boil and add the arugula. Turn off the heat. Add one ladle of the water used to cook the pasta.

Drain the pasta and add it to the frying pan ingredients and mix well. Add 1 tablespoon Parmesan cheese and mix well.

Serve in bowls and top each serving with a sprinkle of extra virgin olive oil and Parmesan cheese.

Note: Arugula is a nutty, peppery green, which will give this pasta sauce a little kick.

Variations: You can substitute spinach, escarole, or broccoli for the arugula.
You can substitute shrimp or pancetta for the prosciutto.
You can substitute spaghetti or any pasta for the penne.

PASTA WITH SEAFOOD
>MAKARONIA THALASINA

INGREDIENTS

3 Cloves garlic, sliced thin
1 Tablespoon fresh flat -leaf
parsley, chopped finely
1 Tablespoon fresh thyme,
chopped finely
1 Cup dry, white wine
Freshly ground pepper to taste
2 Tablespoons extra virgin olive oil
1 Pound of spaghetti or penne pasta

This dish can be made with Octopus, Clams, Mussels, Shrimp, calamari or sepia.

Be sure that you have cleaned and washed the shellfish well. If you choose to use octopus, use baby octopus; it will be soft and tender. You can find it frozen in many Asian markets.

Bring a large pot of water to a boil. Add 1 teaspoon of salt. Add the pasta and cook until it is al dente; drain well.

In a large saucepan, sauté the garlic until it is golden brown. Remove the garlic and set aside. Add the wine, parsley, thyme, and seafood of your choice, Cover and cook until the shellfish are open or the shrimp is pink (but not tough). If you are using calamari or sepia, cook until just soft. Do not overcook them or they will be tough. Add a ladle of the pasta water and stir well.

Serving suggestions: Use a large, flat soup bowl. Put the pasta in the bowl and ladle the seafood and sauce over the pasta. Add fresh pepper and sprinkle with chopped parsley.

Variation:
½ cup of well-washed leeks, cut into strips
1 red pepper, seeded and cut into strips
Sauté the leeks and peppers in olive oil over a high heat until soft. Drain and arrange over the top of the seafood pasta.

TOASTED COUSCOUS
>PSITO COUSCOUS

INGREDIENTS

2 Cups couscous
1 Shallot, finely minced
1 Tablespoon butter or extra virgin olive oil
1 Tablespoon fresh mint, chopped finely
1 Tablespoon fresh flat-leaf parsley, chopped finely
1 Cup low-fat, low-sodium chicken broth (optional)

Couscous is a pasta dish served all over the Mediterranean.

In a two-quart saucepan, sauté the shallot in butter or olive oil over a medium flame until it is translucent. Add the couscous and sauté until the couscous is lightly browned (about five minutes). Slowly add 2 cups of boiling water (or 1 cup each water and chicken broth) and bring to a boil. Reduce the heat to medium-low and cover. Simmer for 12 minutes or until the liquid is absorbed. Add the mint and parsley, and stir together.

Variations: Add ½ cup of zucchini, carrots, red or yellow peppers (coarsely diced), green onions (diagonally diced). Add 1 cup toasted slivered almonds, or ½ cup pine nuts. Add ½ cup wild mushrooms sautéed in butter or olive oil.

Serving suggestions: Serve with roasted or grilled meats and fish. It is also an excellent alternative to summer salads and side dishes made with fresh vegetables.

SHRIMP AND HEARTS OF ARTICHOKE WITH PASTA
>MAKARONIA ME GARIDES KE AGINARES

INGREDIENTS

36 Medium to large shrimp
¼ Pounds pancetta,
chopped coarsely
2 Cans artichoke hearts
2 Large Roma tomatoes, peeled,
seeded, and chopped coarsely
1 Cup fresh basil, chopped, coarsely
1 Cup fresh parsley,
chopped coarsely
1 Teaspoon fresh thyme,
chopped finely
½ Cup dry white wine
1 Teaspoon fresh lemon juice
6 Cloves garlic, sliced thinly
2 Tablespoons extra virgin olive oil
1 Tablespoon butter
8 Ounces Parmesan or Kefalotyri
cheese, grated
Sea salt and freshly
ground black pepper
1 Pound package thin spaghetti

Bring a large pot of water to a boil. Add 1 teaspoon of sea salt. Add the pasta and cook until it is al dente. Drain well.

Peel and devein the shrimp, leaving the tails on. In a large skillet, render the pancetta and reserve the fat. Cook the pancetta until crisp, and drain on paper towels. Drain the artichoke hearts and cut them in half. In the same skillet, add the olive oil and brown the garlic until it is golden brown. Remove the garlic and set aside. Add the shrimp and cook them over a very hot fire for 30 seconds. And the tomatoes and artichoke hearts; continue cooking the shrimp until they are pink. Add the white wine and cook for 1 minute or until the wine evaporates. Add the butter and lemon and stir.

Serve the pasta in individual bowls and top with the shrimp and artichokes. Sprinkle the pancetta and golden garlic over the dish; top with grated cheese.

SAUCES
& STOCKS

SALTSA KE ZOMOS

LEFKAS COUNTRY-STYLE MEAT SAUCE
>LEFKAS PASTITSADA

INGREDIENTS

4 Tablespoons extra virgin olive oil
2 Very large sweet onions, peeled
and diced coarsely
2 Garlic cloves, chopped finely
3 Tablespoon fresh flat-leaf
parsley, chopped finely
3 Sprigs fresh thyme
2 Pounds very lean ground pork
1 Pound ground veal
½ Cup dry white wine
6 Large tomatoes, seeded and
chopped finely
1 Tablespoon tomato paste
5 Whole cloves
¼ Teaspoon nutmeg
1 Large stick cinnamon
2 Tablespoons all-purpose flour
1 Tablespoon fresh basil, torn
into bite-sized pieces
Salt and freshly ground
pepper to taste
6 Cups water

Heat 3 tablespoons of the olive oil in a large saucepan over medium heat; sauté the onions for about 5 minutes, or until the onions are translucent. Sprinkle with flour and continue cooking for a minute. Add the white wine, tomatoes, tomato paste, cinnamon, nutmeg, cloves, thyme, salt, and pepper, and sauté for 5 minutes. Transfer this mixture to a bowl and reserve.
Sauté the ground meat in the same saucepan, stirring constantly, for about 10 minutes or until the meat has browned. Add the onion mixture and the water and stir well. Bring the mixture to a boil for 5 to 10 minutes. Then simmer the sauce for 45 to 60 minutes or until the sauce has thickened.
(Makes 5 cups.)

Serving suggestion: Serve over thin spaghetti. Use grated Kefalotyri cheese and basil to garnish.

MEAT SAUCE WITH WILD MUSHROOMS
>KYMAS ME AGRIA MANITARIA

INGREDIENTS

2½ Pounds ground leg of veal
2 Pounds ground sirloin
½ Pound ground pork
4 Strips bacon, sliced thick, cut in 1-Inch pieces
4 Strips pancetta, cut in 1-inch pieces
1 Large sweet or Spanish onion, chopped finely
1 Shallot, chopped finely
3 Tablespoons flat-leaf parsley, chopped finely
3 Tablespoons grated carrots
1 Tablespoon butter
1 Bay leaf
2 Tablespoons chopped celery
4 Dry shiitake mushrooms
4 Dry porcini mushrooms
1 Can whole tomatoes, chopped finely (save the juice)
6 Fresh Roma tomatoes, chopped
2 Tablespoons tomato paste (Kyknos brand preferred.)
4 Cups water
½ Cup milk
1 Teaspoon lemon zest
¼ Teaspoon nutmeg

Reconstitute the mushrooms by soaking them in hot water for 10 minutes. Render the bacon and pancetta until well done. Remove and reserve the bacon. Brown the meat in the bacon fat. In a separate pan, place 1 tablespoon of butter, onion, celery, bay leaf, mushrooms, carrots, and 2 tablespoons of the parsley, and cook five minutes, or until the onion is translucent. Add to the meat. Add nutmeg, tomatoes, tomato paste, and water. Stir well; bring the sauce to a boil and cook, covered, for two hours over medium heat. When the sauce is done, turn off the heat and add the milk. Remove the bay leaf.

Serving suggestions: Serve over spaghetti, fettuccine, or linguine.

Chef's trick: When the bowls are heaped with pasta and sauce, sprinkle the tablespoon of flat-leaf parsley and the lemon zest on top.

MEAT SAUCE WITH GREEK SPICES >ELINIKOS KYMAS

INGREDIENTS

4 Tablespoons olive oil
2 Medium yellow onions, peeled and diced
2 Garlic cloves, chopped finely
2 Celery stalks, diced
3 Tablespoons fresh flat-leaf parsley, chopped finely
3 Sprigs fresh thyme
2 Pounds very lean ground beef
½ Cup red wine
½ Cup dry white wine
12 Ripe Roma tomatoes (roasted), chopped finely
1 Tablespoon tomato paste
1 Teaspoon allspice
½ Stick of cinnamon
2 Bay leaves
Salt and freshly ground pepper to taste
6 Cups of water

Heat 3 tablespoons of the olive oil in a large saucepan over medium heat; sauté the onions, garlic, celery, parsley, oregano, and thyme for about 5 minutes, or until the onions are translucent. Transfer this mixture to a bowl and reserve.

Sauté the ground beef in the same saucepan, stirring constantly, for about 10 minutes, or until the meat has browned. Add the red and white wine, tomatoes, tomato paste, cinnamon, allspice, bay leaves, and salt and pepper; sauté for another 5 minutes. Return the onion, garlic, and celery mix; add the 6 cups of water and stir well. Bring the mixture to a boil for 5 to 10 minutes. Simmer the sauce for 45 to 60 minutes or until the sauce has thickened.

(Makes 5 cups.)

SIMPLE MEAT SAUCE
>KYMAS

INGREDIENTS

4 Tablespoons of olive oil
2 Medium yellow onions
peeled and diced
2 Garlic cloves, chopped finely
2 Celery stalks, peeled and diced
3 Tablespoons of chopped finely
fresh flat-leaf parsley
3 Sprig fresh thyme
2 Pounds very lean ground beef
½ Cup red wine
½ Cup dry white wine
12 Ripe Roma tomatoes (roasted),
chopped finely
1 Tablespoon of tomato paste
1 Teaspoon allspice
½ Stick cinnamon
2 Bay leaves
Salt and freshly ground
pepper to taste
6 Cups of water

Heat 3 tablespoons of the olive oil in a large saucepan over medium heat; sauté the onions, garlic, celery, parsley, oregano, and thyme for about 5 minutes, or until the onions are translucent. Transfer this mixture to a bowl and reserve.

Sauce the ground beef in the same saucepan, stirring constantly, for about 10 minutes or until the meat has browned. Add the red and white wine, tomatoes, tomato paste, cinnamon, allspice, bay leaves, salt and pepper and sauté for another 5 minutes. Return the onion, garlic and celery mix. Add the 6 cups of water. Stir well. Bring the mixture to a boil for 5-10 minutes. Then simmer the sauce for 45 to 60 minutes or until the sauce has thickened. (Makes 5 cups.)

QUICK TOMATO SAUCE
>SALTSA TOMATAS

INGREDIENTS

5 Tablespoons extra virgin olive oil
1 Clove garlic, sliced thinly
Several sprigs thyme or
basil tied together
2 Pounds Roma tomatoes,
skinned, seeded,
and chopped finely
Salt and freshly ground
black pepper

Brown the garlic in the olive oil over a medium fire. Remove the garlic. Add tomatoes and thyme or basil. Season to taste. Allow to simmer on a low fire for 40 minutes, or until the sauce thickens. Add water if needed. Remove the thyme or basil. Before serving, sprinkle the sauce with a little chopped fresh basil or thyme.

Chef's tricks:

1. It is easier to remove the fresh herbs from the pot if you tie them together before putting them in the sauce.
2. A clove of garlic is easy to peel if you put it under a large knife blade and smash the blade with your fist.
3. If you leave the garlic in the sauce, it will make the sauce bitter.
4. Always taste your sauce before serving. Tomatoes have a lot of acid; you may need to add a tiny bit of sugar.
5. Greeks often use a combination of ½ teaspoon thyme, ¼ teaspoon cinnamon, ¼ teaspoon nutmeg and ¼ teaspoon allspice in their tomato sauce.

RAW TOMATO AND BASIL SAUCE
>FRESKIA SALTSA ME VASILIKO

INGREDIENTS

2 Pounds of Roma tomatoes
2 Cloves garlic,
peeled and minced
¼ Cup fresh basil leaves,
torn into small pieces
½ Cup extra virgin olive oil
Coarse sea salt and freshly
ground pepper to taste
1 Tablespoon capers

If the skin of the tomatoes is particularly tough, plunge them into boiling water for 5 seconds. Peel, core, seed, and dice the tomatoes. Combine the garlic, basil, olive oil, and capers in a bowl, and add to the tomatoes. Season the sauce with salt and pepper. Marinate for 1 hour before using. Serve with grilled fish.

ROASTED TOMATO SAUCE
>SALSA TOMATAS TOUFOURNOU

INGREDIENTS

12 Ripe Roma tomatoes cut in half
Extra virgin olive oil
4 Sprigs fresh basil, tied together
2 Cloves garlic
¼ Teaspoon sugar
Salt and pepper

Place the tomato halves in a flat baking dish, skin side down. Sprinkle with olive oil and place in a 400-degree oven until they are soft and slightly blackened on the edges. This should take about 20 minutes.

Remove from the oven and set aside to cool. Remove the skin and chop the tomatoes coarsely.

Sauté garlic in olive oil until lightly browned. Remove the garlic. Add the tomatoes and the basil. Add the sugar and ½ cup water. Cook over a medium fire for 30 minutes or until the sauce thickens. Remove the basil. Add salt and pepper to taste.

Put into a food processor with the metal blade; puree.

Chef's trick: Do not let the garlic get too brown, as this will make the oil bitter.

WHITE BUTTER SAUCE
>ASPRI SALTSA VOUTIROU

INGREDIENTS

¼ Cup shallots, minced finely
1 Teaspoon dried tarragon
6 Tablespoons
champagne vinegar
6 Tablespoons white wine
3 Sticks unsalted butter, cold and
cut into 1-inch pieces
Salt and pepper to taste
1 Tablespoon fresh tarragon,
chopped finely
2–3 Tablespoons fresh parsley,
chopped finely
1 Teaspoon fresh chives,
chopped finely

In a non-reactive pan, cook the shallots, vinegar, and wine over a low heat for 10 minutes. Increase the heat and reduce rapidly until the pan is almost dry. Over a low heat, whisk in the cold butter a little at a time and it becomes a white cream. When the butter is incorporated, add the salt, pepper, and fresh herbs.

Serving suggestions: This sauce is delicious with fresh raw oysters. It can also be used with sautéed fish.

WHITE CREAM SAUCE
>BÉCHAMEL SAUCE

INGREDIENTS

4 Cups milk
2 Bay leaves
8 Tablespoons butter
1 Cup all-purpose flour
3 Tablespoons grated Kefalotyri
or Parmesan cheese
½ Teaspoon nutmeg

Scald the milk and bay leaves in a saucepan over moderate fire. In a separate saucepan, melt the butter, add the flour, and whisk for about five minutes or until combined and a very light brown color develops. Remove the bay leaves from the milk. Slowly pour the milk into the butter mixture; whisk continuously until the sauce reaches the desired thickness. Allow to cool for five minutes. Add the cheese and nutmeg.

Chef's trick: The Greek chefs sometimes add ½ teaspoon allspice berries or a bay leaf to the milk while it is heating. Be sure to remove them before pouring the milk into the butter and flour mixture.

GARLIC (AIOLI) MAYONNAISE SAUCE
>SALTSA ME MAYONEZA KE SCORDO

INGREDIENTS

**1/3 Cup stale breadcrumbs from
white unsweetened bread
2-4 Tablespoons red wine vinegar
6-8 Cloves garlic, pressed
½ Teaspoon salt
6 Egg yolks
1 ½ to 2 Cups olive oil
½ Teaspoon Cayenne pepper**

Moisten breadcrumbs with a tablespoon or two of vinegar and place in a food processor. Pulse several times or until it forms a paste that is smooth. Add the salt and 2 of the egg yolks and process until the mixture is very thick and sticky. Begin to add the olive oil very slowly until the sauce is thick and heavy. Thin out with a few drops of vinegar. Season with salt and pepper to taste. Add the rest of the egg yolks and process until smooth.

GREEN SAUCE
>PRASINI SALTSA

INGREDIENTS

**1 Cup flat-leaf parsley, minced
2 Garlic cloves,
peeled and minced
2 Tablespoons capers,
coarsely chopped
2 to 4 Canned flat anchovy
fillets, minced
½ Cup lemon juice
¾ Cup extra virgin olive oil**

In a small bowl, mix together the parsley, garlic, capers, and enough minced anchovy to give the sauce a salted punch. Stir in the lemon juice and olive oil. Mix thoroughly. Cover tightly with plastic wrap and refrigerate for up to 1 week.

Variations: You may substitute vinegar for the lemon juice.

Serving suggestions: This sauce is delicious with poached fish or roasted meats. This sauce is used for meats.

WILD GAME BIRD SAUCE
>SALTSA GIA AGRIOPOULIA

INGREDIENTS

**Bones and trimmings
from the de-boned fowl
1 Shallot, unpeeled and cut in half
2 Pearl onions,
unpeeled and cut in quarters
2 Cloves garlic, unpeeled
and cut in half.
1 Carrot, washed but not peeled,
and cut into 2-inch pieces
1 Stalk of celery, cut into
2-Inch pieces
2 Sprigs thyme
1 Roma tomato, quartered
1 Tablespoon all-purpose flour
4 Whole peppercorns
1 Cup veal stock
1 Cup chicken stock
1 Cup water
½ Cup dry white wine
2 Tablespoons extra virgin olive oil**

This sauce can be used for pheasant, quail, squab, woodcock, or pigeon. It is also the base for sauces used with duck.

In a saucepan over a hot fire, sauté the bones and trimmings in olive oil. Add the vegetables and herbs and cook until they are browned. Add the white wine and cook until it evaporates (2 to 3 minutes). Sprinkle a tablespoon of flour over the mixture and stir. Add the veal stock, chicken stock, and water. Bring to a boil. Turn the heat down and let the pot simmer for 45 minutes. Strain the sauce and toss out the vegetables and bones. Return the sauce to the pot and reduce by half. You should have about 1½ cups of sauce.

If you are using this base for duck, add 1 tablespoon of orange marmalade or 1 tablespoon of either cherry or blackberry preserves.

PESTO
>SALTSA VASILIKOU

INGREDIENTS

3 Bunches basil, well rinsed
1 Bunch flat-leaf parsley,
well rinsed
1 Bunch chives
¼ Cup Parmagiano Reggiano or
Kefalotyri cheese, grated finely
2 Tablespoons goat cheese
2 Tablespoons toasted pine nuts
Pinch red pepper flakes
Freshly ground black
pepper and salt to taste
1 Cup extra virgin olive oil

Combine all the ingredients except the olive oil in a food processor; with the motor running, slowly pour in the oil. Process until smooth.
Makes about 1¾ cups.

GARLIC AND POTATO DIPPING SAUCE
>POURE APO PATATES KE SKORDO

INGREDIENTS

1 Whole head garlic
6 Large Yukon Gold potatoes
1 Teaspoon salt
Fresh-ground white pepper
1 Cup extra virgin olive oil
½ Cup red wine vinegar

Wrap a whole head of garlic in foil and put it in a skillet in a preheated oven at 400 degrees for 30 minutes. Remove the foil and cut the top off. Allow it to cool.
Peel the potatoes. Bring them to a boil in a large pot. Cook the potatoes for 20 minutes or until they are soft in the middle. Drain them.
Place each potato in a ricer and squeeze into a food processor. Add the olive oil and vinegar slowly until the mixture is creamy. Add, salt, and pepper, and mix well. If the potatoes are a bit thick, add more extra virgin olive oil until you have the desired consistency. When the garlic is easy to handle, squeeze the roasted garlic into the potato mixture. Mix well.

EGG LEMON SAUCE
>AVGOLEMONO SALTSA

INGREDIENTS

Yolks of four eggs
Salt and pepper to taste
1 Cup of hot water or
vegetable broth
5 Tablespoons butter
Juice of 1½ lemons
1 Tablespoon corn starch

This is the most famous of the Greek sauces and is used in many dishes.

Beat the egg yolks very well; add the lemon juice and cornstarch, and beat thoroughly. Slowly pour in a cup of liquid, either hot water or vegetable broth, beating all the while, until the sauce thickens.

Chef's trick: This sounds like an old wives tale, but it works. While beating the sauce, make a kissing sound with your lips. This will help keep the sauce from breaking.

VEAL STOCK
>ZOMOS MOSXARION

INGREDIENTS

3 Bay leaves
Salt and pepper
1 Full head of garlic,
cut in half horizontally
6 Pounds veal bones
3 Pounds chicken bones
1 Large Spanish or yellow onion,
unpeeled and quartered
2 Large carrots, peeled and cut
into 2-inch pieces
2 Celery stalks (including the
leaves), chopped
2 Leeks (both green and white
parts), washed and chopped

While it is time-consuming to make your own stock, it is worth the effort. It takes 8 to 10 hours. This is an essential for Greek cuisine. It is the basis for many of the stews and brown sauces. I make it once a month in large quantities and freeze it in small plastic containers for future use.

Season the bones with salt and pepper and place them in a roasting pan in a hot oven (400 to 500 degrees); roast them for 1½ hours. Turn the bones during cooking to ensure that all sides are well browned. Add the vegetables and roast for the last 30 minutes.
In a large stockpot, bring 2 gallons of water to a boil and add the roasted bones, bay leaves, and vegetables. Bring the liquid back to a boil; reduce the heat to a slow simmer and cook for 6–8 hours. In restaurants, it is common to simmer the stock for 24 hours.
Strain the broth and set it aside to cool.

HEALTHY CHICKEN STOCK
>IGIINOS ZOMOS KOTAS

INGREDIENTS

1 Large hen, 4–5 pounds
2 Onions,
unpeeled and quartered
2 Celery stalks,
cut into 2-inch pieces
2 Carrots, peeled and cut into 2-
Inch pieces
4 Cloves garlic
1 Leek, washed well and cut into
2-Inch pieces
4 Sprigs fresh thyme
3 Bay leaves
4 Sprigs fresh parsley
1 Tablespoon peppercorns

Wash the chicken well and place it in a stockpot. Add 4 quarts of water and bring it to a boil for 1 hour. Skim the surface frequently. In a shallow baking dish, put the onions, carrots, garlic, and celery. Place in a preheated oven for 30 minutes at 350 degrees. Add all of the other ingredients to the stockpot and reduce the heat to simmer. When the vegetables are roasted, add them to the stockpot and simmer for 2 hours. Cool the broth and strain it. Place the broth in the refrigerator overnight. Remove the fat that has risen to the top with a large spoon.

Chef's trick: In a good kitchen supply store, you can find a de-fat cup. Pour the broth into the cup and let it rest a minute. The fat will rise to the top and you can pour the de-fatted broth through the tube at the bottom. This is a real time saver.

FISH STOCK
>ZOMOS PSARION

INGREDIENTS

4 Pounds fish heads and bones
1 Leek, washed well and
chopped coarsely
1 Large carrot,
peeled and chopped
4 Celery stalks, chopped
1 Large yellow onion, quartered
1 Fennel bulb, quartered
2 Cups white wine
1 Head garlic,
cut in half horizontally
4 Lemons, halved
6 Sprigs fresh thyme
1 Large bunch fresh Italian
flat-leaf parsley
1 Tablespoon peppercorns
8 Quarts water

Remove the gills and the eyes from the fish heads. Put the fish heads and bones, vegetables, and herbs in a large stockpot with 8 quarts of water; bring to a boil. Reduce the heat and cook for 30 minutes. Strain and discard the bones, vegetables, and herbs.

DESSERTS

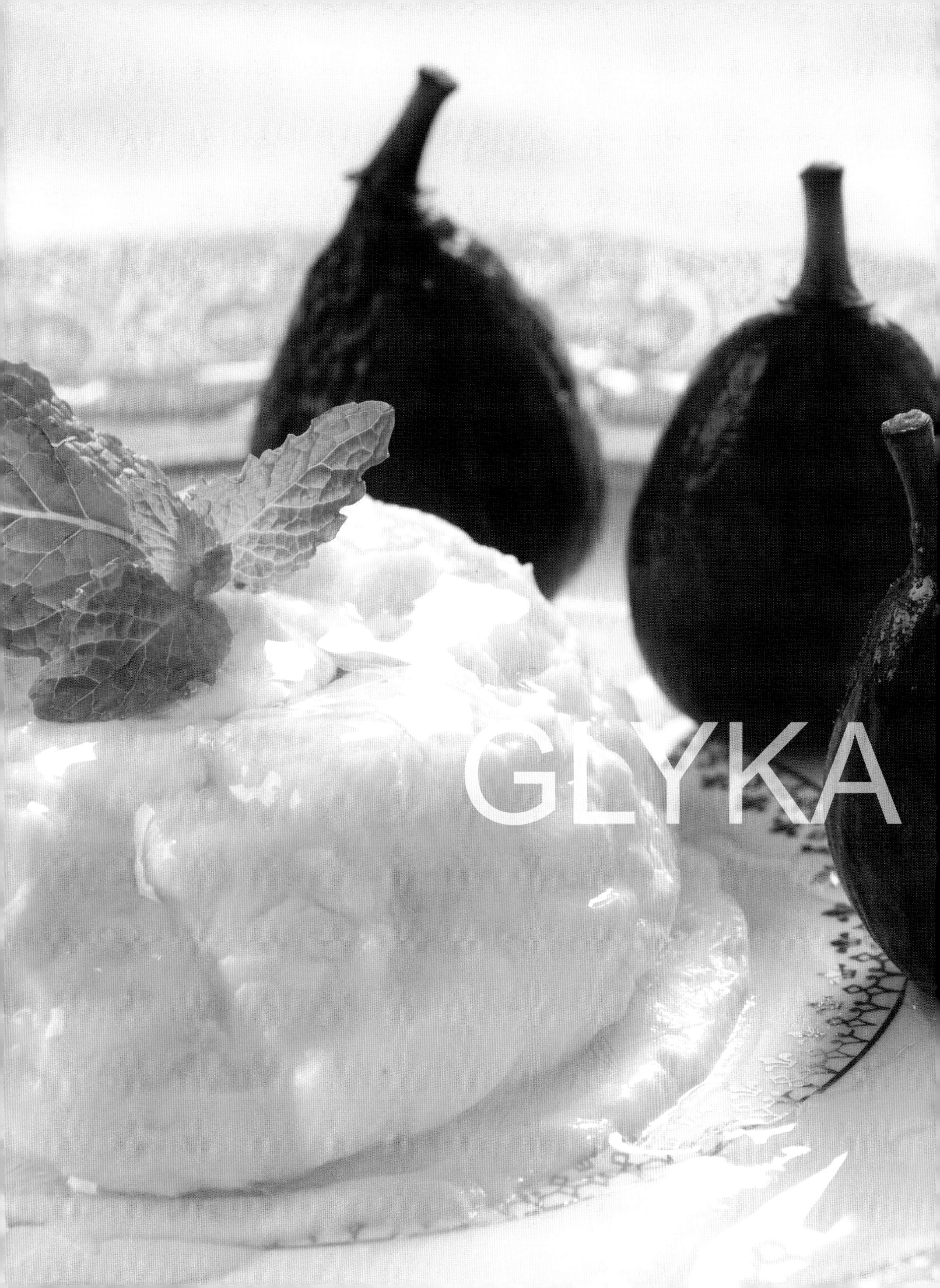

GLYKA

SPOON SWEETS
>GLYKA TOU KOUTALIOU

INGREDIENTS

**2 Pounds sour cherries
(or other fruits, such as figs or
Seville oranges)**

SYRUP:
2 Cups sugar
½ Cup thyme honey
2½ Cups water
**1 Strip lemon zest or 2
tablespoons strained lemon juice**

Wash and stone the cherries in a large bowl so that all the juices are preserved. In the case of the oranges, only the peel is used. In the case of the figs, they are kept whole.

Place the fruit and its juices, sugar, lemon, honey, and water into a saucepan. Bring to a boil. Let simmer for 10 to 15 minutes, skimming off any froth with a slotted spoon.

Remove the fruit with a slotted spoon into a bowl. Then transfer to sterilized canning jars. Continue to boil the syrup until it thickens. Pour the syrup over the fruit. While the mixture is hot, tighten the lids well and turn upside down overnight. Check that the lids are on tight. Store in a cool place.

Serve with Greek yogurt or alone on a small plate.

CRISP HONEY DOUGHNUTS
>LOUKOUMADES

INGREDIENTS

3 Envelopes yeast
3 Cups warm water
4 ½ Cups all purpose flour
½ Teaspoon salt
Corn oil for deep frying
2 Teaspoons cinnamon
6 Tablespoons thyme-scented
Greek honey

Dissolve the yeast in warm water. Add salt and flour. Mix well until a loose dough is formed. Cover with a towel and keep in a warm place until it doubles in bulk. While the dough is rising, warm up the honey for 1 minute. Keep warm.

Heat oil in a stockpot. When it is just under the smoking point, drop a teaspoon of the mixture into the oil, about six at a time. Dip the teaspoon in cool water between each batch to prevent the dough from sticking. The doughnuts will puff up and rise to the surface within seconds. Turn them with a slotted spoon. When they acquire a pale golden color, lift them out with a slotted spoon and drain on a paper towel. Drizzle the honey over them and sprinkle with the cinnamon.

ALMOND COOKIES
>KOURABIEDES

INGREDIENTS

1½ Cups whole almonds, peeled
2 Cups butter, softened
1 Cup sugar
3 Egg yolks
½ Cup ouzo (or brandy)
Seeds from one vanilla pod
(or 1 teaspoon vanilla extract)
8½ Cups all-purpose flour
2 Teaspoons baking powder
Pinch of salt
4 Tablespoons rose water
Confectioner's sugar

On the island of Lefkas, these cookies are made for all festive occasions.

Preheat the oven to 375 degrees. Place the almonds on a baking sheet and roast in the oven; remove and let them cool. Place the almonds in a food processor and chop them finely. Cream the butter and sugar together in a large bowl. Add the eggs, brandy, and vanilla seeds. Sift the flour, salt, and baking powder into the bowl. Add the almonds and mix together well.
On a cold surface, sprinkle flour and place the mixture on top. Knead the mixture by hand into smooth dough. Roll it out until it is under ½ inch thick. Use a biscuit cutter or the rim of a small glass to cut out semi-circles and arrange them on a greased baking sheet. Place in the oven for about 20 minutes. Cool the cookies on a rack. Sprinkle them with rose water and confectioner's sugar.

BAKED QUINCES
>KYTHONI TOUFOURNOU

INGREDIENTS

3 Pounds quinces
2 Cups sugar
1 Large cinnamon stick
Several whole cloves
3 Cups water

Preheat the oven to 350 degrees. Wash the quinces and cut in half. Remove the seeds and the core. In a large saucepan, add the sugar, cinnamon, seeds, cores, and water; boil for 10 minutes. Stick the cloves into each half of a quince. Place in an ovenproof ceramic baking dish. Strain the juice and pour over the quinces. Cook for 1 to 1½ hours.

Serving suggestions: When cold, the baked quinces are best served with creme freche or whipped cream.

Variations: Blanched and toasted almonds can be sprinkled over this dish.

ALEXIS' CHEESECAKE
>TOURTA TYRIOU

INGREDIENTS

3 8 Ounce packages Philadelphia
cream cheese
1 Cup sugar
4 Eggs
1 Teaspoon vanilla extract
1 Pint sour cream
1 Box Zwieback
(crush in blender to make crumbs)

Cream the cheese with ½ cup sugar and the vanilla. Fold in the eggs one at a time. (This makes the cake lighter.) Use margarine on a paper towel to grease the pan. Press the Zwieback crumbs into the pan to form a crust. Pour the cream cheese mixture into the crust. Bake in the oven for 30 minutes at 350 degrees.
Combine the sour cream and ½ cup sugar. Beat it with a wire whisk for 3 minutes. Put it on top of the cake and put back in the oven for 10 minutes.
Refrigerate for a few hours before serving.

SPICED COOKIES
>MELOMAKOROUNA

INGREDIENTS

3 Tablespoons extra virgin olive oil
1 Cup canola oil
¼ Cup sugar
½ Cup beer
1/3 Cup brandy
¼ Cup orange zest
1 Teaspoon ground cinnamon
½ Teaspoon ground cloves
¼ Teaspoon ground nutmeg
1 Teaspoon baking soda
2 Teaspoon baking powder
1 Cup peeled, toasted, ground almonds
3 Cups all-purpose flour
4 Tablespoons butter
6 Tablespoons shortening
Zest and juice of one medium orange

SYRUP:
1½ Cups honey
3 Cups sugar
1 Cinnamon stick
2 Cups water
10 Whole cloves
Juice of ½ lemon

SPRINKLE:
1 Tablespoon of finely chopped almonds mixed with 1 teaspoon cinnamon and a teaspoon of sugar over the cookies.

Sift the flour, baking powder, baking soda, and salt together into a medium bowl.

In a separate bowl, beat the butter and shortening together until creamy with a Kitchen Aid mixer with the dough attachment. Use a high speed. While that is still beating, add the olive oil, canola oil, and the sugar. Add the nutmeg, cloves, cinnamon and orange zest. Add the beer and the brandy and continue beating. Add the flour mixture in several batches. When the dough forms, roll it out on a floured cold surface. Form a ball with the dough and place it in a bowl covered with a towel and let it rest to rise for a half hour in a warm place.

Combine the chopped nuts and honey for the filling.

Flour the cold surface again and knead the dough for a few minutes. Make a roll of the dough and cut into 2-inch sections. Shape each piece into an oblong. Use your finger to make an indentation. Add a little of the filling and press the dough to cover it.

Preheat the oven to 350°. Place the cookies on an ungreased cookie sheet and bake them for 20 minutes. Allow them to cool.

While the cookies are baking, make the syrup. Combine all of the syrup ingredients and boil them for 10 minutes. When the cookies are cool, dip them in the syrup and sprinkle them with ground walnuts. Place them on a platter to serve.

HONEY AND WALNUTS IN PHYLLO
>BAKLAVAS

INGREDIENTS

½ Cup chopped walnuts and almonds mixed and ground fine
4 Tablespoons sugar
1 Teaspoon cinnamon
1 Cup butter
1 Package phyllo dough

SYRUP:
1 Cup granulated sugar
7 Tablespoons thyme honey
2 Cloves
1 Bay leaf
1 Cinnamon stick
Juice of ½ lemon
Water

Preheat the oven to 350 degrees. Mix the nuts with the sugar and cinnamon. Melt the butter. Grease the bottom of a large baking dish. Keep the phyllo under damp, clean dishtowels until ready to use. Place two sheets of phyllo in the bottom. Brush the pastry leaves with butter. Cover the top layer with nuts and cinnamon filling. Repeat until you have stacked 8 layers. Top with two sheets of pasty and brush with melted butter. Trim off any excess pastry from the edges. Using a wet knife blade, cut into triangles. Sprinkle with water and bake for 30–40 minutes.

Boil the sugar in 6 cups of water for 5 minutes. Add the honey, cloves, cinnamon, bay leaf, and lemon. Bring to a boil and put it in the refrigerator to cool.
Pour the syrup over the warm pastry. Note: The syrup must be cool before you pour it over the warm pastry.

Variations: You can substitute pistachio nuts or almonds for walnuts.

FRIED DOUGH WITH HONEY AND CINNAMON
>TIGANITES

INGREDIENTS

1½ Cups all-purpose flour
1/2 Teaspoon salt
Corn oil

This is a 15-minute dessert that can be served in many variations.

Into a mixing bowl, put 1½ cup of all-purpose flour and salt. Mix in cold water with a wire whisk until you reach the consistency of pancake batter. Put 1½ inches of corn oil in a large frying pan and heat over a medium flame. When the oil is hot, use a tablespoon to drop dollops of the batter into the oil. Working with a slotted spoon, turn the tiganites once when one side is golden brown. Remove them from the oil and drain for 1 minute on a paper towel. Serve a batch of these piled high on a plate; drizzle honey over them. Sprinkle them lightly with cinnamon and serve them warm.

Variations:
1. Instead of honey, sprinkle the warm tiganites with granulated sugar.
2. Make a pile of tiganites by adding a layer of Greek yogurt between each one. Top with honey and cinnamon.
3. Make a pile of tiganites by adding a layer of vanilla ice cream between each one. Top with honey and cinnamon.
4. Make a pile of tiganites by adding a layer of Greek yogurt and fresh berries between each one. Top with honey and cinnamon. Note: Many kinds of berries can be used, such as strawberries, blackberries, raspberries, or blueberries.
5. Make a pile of tiganites by adding a layer of Greek yogurt and a spoon sweet between each one. Top with cinnamon. Note: The syrup from the spoon sweets can be substituted for the honey.

CUSTARD IN PHYLLO
>GALAKTOBOUREKO

INGREDIENTS

CUSTARD:
6 Cups milk
3 Eggs at room temperature, beaten well
1 Cup granulated sugar
½ Cup butter
1 Cup farina
1 Package phyllo
2 Sticks melted butter

SYRUP:
2 Cups sugar
½ Cup thyme honey
2 Cups water
1 Strip lemon zest or 2 tablespoons strained lemon juice
Custard:

In a large saucepan, combine the sugar and milk and bring to a boil. Gradually add the farina and the butter, and stir constantly with a wooden spoon over a medium heat until the custard has thickened. Turn off the heat and add the eggs, while stirring well.

Preheat the oven to 350 degrees. Line a greased baking pan with 8 to 10 sheets of phyllo; brush each sheet with melted butter before stacking the next sheet on top of it; this will keep the pastry flaky. Pour in the custard and top with 6 to 8 sheets of phyllo, again brushing each individual sheet with melted butter. Using a sharp knife, dip the knife in lukewarm water and score the top sheets of phyllo. Do not score the custard. Bake the galaktoboureko for about 30 minutes, or until the phyllo is golden.

Set aside to cool. When the syrup is still warm, but not hot, pour it over the custard and phyllo.

Syrup: In a medium saucepan, boil the sugar, honey, lemon, and water for ten minutes.

Syrup variations: The recipe for syrup used in Greek desserts varies widely. Some housewives prefer to use orange instead of lemon; some add cinnamon and cloves; others add a tablespoon of brandy. Some use honey and others use only sugar; it is a matter of taste.

Chef's trick: Use a sharp knife to test this dish for doneness. It is perfectly cooked if it comes out perfectly clean when you plunge the knife in.

INDEX >ENGLISH

INDEX > GREEK